# THE GREAT CIRCUS PARADE

by
Herbert Clement & Dominique Jando
photography by
Tom Nebbia

Gareth Stevens Publishing
Milwaukee

The Great Circus Parade
© Copyright The Guidebook Company Ltd., 1989

Library of Congress Cataloging-in-Publication Data

Clement, Herbert
    The great circus parade/Herbert Clement & Dominique Jando;
    photography by Tom Nebbia.        p.        cm.
    Includes index.
    ISBN 0-8368-0156-3
    1.  Great Circus Parade, Milwaukee, Wis.—History. I. Jando,
Dominique, 1945−    . II. Nebbia, Tom.  III. Title.
GV1819.C58            1989            89-4538
791.3′8′0977595—dc20

North American edition first published in 1989 by

Gareth Stevens, Inc.
7317 W. Green Tree Road
Milwaukee, Wisconsin, 53223 USA

Text copyright © 1989 by Herbert Clement and
Dominique Jando
Photography copyright © 1989 by Tom Nebbia
Additional photography by Magnus Bartlett and Zane B. Williams
Design and artwork by Joan Law Design & Photography

Printed in Hong Kong

1 2 3 4 5 6 7 8 9 95 94 93 92 91 90 89

*Exoticism in rural America: This 1913 magazine cover perfectly captures the sense of novelty and excitement brought to towns all over America by the free street parade of visiting circuses. (Courtesy Ladies' Home Journal.)*

*Preceding page: Locked in gilded combat since the 1860s, these adversaries, along with many other elaborate carvings, adorn the magnificent Gladiator Telescoping Tableau Wagon.*

AN ALL-STORY NUMBER

# THE LADIES' HOME JOURNAL

JULY 1913
15 CENTS

THE CURTIS PUBLISHING COMPANY
PHILADELPHIA

*Participants or viewers—who can tell? All of Milwaukee is circus-crazy on parade day!*

*Detail of Gollmar Bros. Circus' Kangaroo Tableau Wagon.*

It is rare, indeed, when an important figure's love of life and love of people can be translated into so much happiness for so many. We salute Ben Barkin who, as a volunteer, produces the Great Circus Parade, and dedicate this book to him. He has proven that if you follow the sound of the calliope, you can't go wrong.

Herbert Clement
Dominique Jando

# CONTENTS

# Acknowledgements

Among the many who helped in the development of this book, the authors wish to thank the following:

Ben Barkin, to whom this book is dedicated, for encouraging the project from its very start; Robert I. Ducas, for his belief and enthusiasm in the project, his perception and his unique ability to pull it all together; Tom Nebbia, whose photographic genius is obvious throughout these pages, for his professional derring-do in the face of snarling circus big cats, stomping elephants and over-excited crowds; Chappie Fox, for contributing his reminiscences, his support, and above all, for having played a vital part in creating the Great Circus Parade; Sallie W. Coolidge, for her editorial expertise and for her transformation from curmudgeon to serious circus enthusiast; Greg Parkinson, Director, Circus World Museum, Baraboo, Wisconsin and Vice-President, Circus Historical Society, for his interest and support; Frederick Fried, whose historical treatise, *Artists in Wood*, was of immeasurable help during this book's research period; Wolf A. Popper, for his help in bringing the project to life; Ed Breisacher and John T. Westlake, for important production support during the early stages of this book's development; Albert McGrigor for editorial advice and criticism; Frank Robie, for the loan of historical material; Chris Kilduff, for making possible the reproduction of historical documents; Margaret Stocker for graphic restoration services; Amy Korenvaes for technical support and moral encouragement; and Alfredo E. Rotsellio. The authors' special thanks go to Magnus Bartlett, not only for photographic contributions, but for falling victim to the magic of the circus parade phenomenon, having the vision of this book's importance, and the initiative to bring the project to fruition. Evelyn Curro's watercolour plates of historic circus wagons are published through the courtesy of the Ringling Museum of Art, Sarasota, Florida.

*Mutual love affair: There is a special feeling between Ben Barkin, producer of the parade, and the hundreds of thousands of spectators.*

# Introduction

The people of Milwaukee have a good sense of history; they strive to preserve the old and combine it creatively with the new for their children. With such a tradition of celebrating history, it is not surprising that they took the Great Circus Parade — an annual event in Milwaukee — into their hearts from its very beginning in 1963. It is a parade that combines art and history — the magnificent wooden wagons in which circuses toured the United States and Europe a century ago — with a need for dramatic, enduring, contemporary entertainment.

And what could be more dramatic than 750 powerful Percherons, Belgians and Clydesdales working as four-, six-, eight- and even ten-horse hitches to draw heavy, rumbling, old circus wagons, each restored to its original majesty and brilliance with bright paints, gilding and mirrors? Add to that spectacle helmeted wagon drivers in brilliant uniforms, skillfully guiding teams down the avenues of downtown Milwaukee with their complicated right- and left-hand turns past hundreds of thousands of citizens who have paced the curbines for hours in anticipation of the event. Add the drama of live tigers, lions and leopards, snakes and monkeys, passing almost within reach of the spectators. And, on top of that, add the spectacular precision of some of the best U.S. military bands, the marching units and the fast beat of the circus bands perched atop grand old band wagons.

New to the parade when it was revived in 1985 (after a twelve-year hiatus) were the ringing tunes of the old Ringling Brothers' bellwagon, which joined the long-familiar shrieking tunes of the calliope, its steam rising in puffy white clouds. In the parade, exotic pedestrians included ungainly camels and ponderous, shuffling elephants bringing up the rear.

These are sounds which can be heard only at the Great Circus Parade in Milwaukee each summer in July. And, too, it is only because of a unique resource, the State of Wisconsin's Historical Society Circus World Museum at Baraboo, Wisconsin, that the parade exists. For the museum's collection of more than 100 old circus wagons is unrivaled.

Putting that collection together in the Great Circus Parade gives old folks something to remember and young people the fun and excitement that the arrival of the circus provided before the age of television and radio. Today, thousands come from the Milwaukee community and more distant environs to view the parade. It is an event that rivals the Mardi Gras in New Orleans, the Indianapolis 500, the Kentucky Derby in

*Costumed participants join parade benefactors on the slow train ride from the Circus World Museum in Baraboo to the parade grounds in Milwaukee.*

Louisville and the Tournament of Roses festival in Pasadena for splendor. In fact, the turnout for the Great Circus Parade — as many as 750,000 — exceeds the turnout for those other events, too.

But perhaps as much as any other factor, what makes this parade unique is the sense of family participation it brings: it is very much a people's parade. In 1985, more than 9,000 contributors sent money — in some cases just a dollar or two — to help out in any way they could. Their names were placed in a drum which in turn was dropped into the "shoe" of the *Old Woman Who Lived In A Shoe* circus wagon. Celebrities from local radio and television stations drew first the finalists and in turn from that selection drew the Grand Marshall of the parade — not a well-known figure, but a member of the community taken at random.

When the 1985 parade was over, many calls and letters came in urging greater local participation in the future. Letters of praise continued to come to the city's two daily newspapers, urging that the parade become an annual event once again.

A very great sense of satisfaction comes from this event, from the fact that it is so heartily received by people, young and old, rich and poor, of all colors and beliefs. They come together for the circus event days and especially for the parade itself. I hope you will find equal satisfaction and pleasure in the pages of this book which convey the variety, beauty and excitement of a very special tradition.

*Each village and hamlet from Baraboo to Milwaukee draws its group of happy admirers when the circus train passes through on its journey from yesterday into tomorrow.*

Ben Barkin
*Producer, the Great Circus Parade,
Milwaukee, Wisconsin*

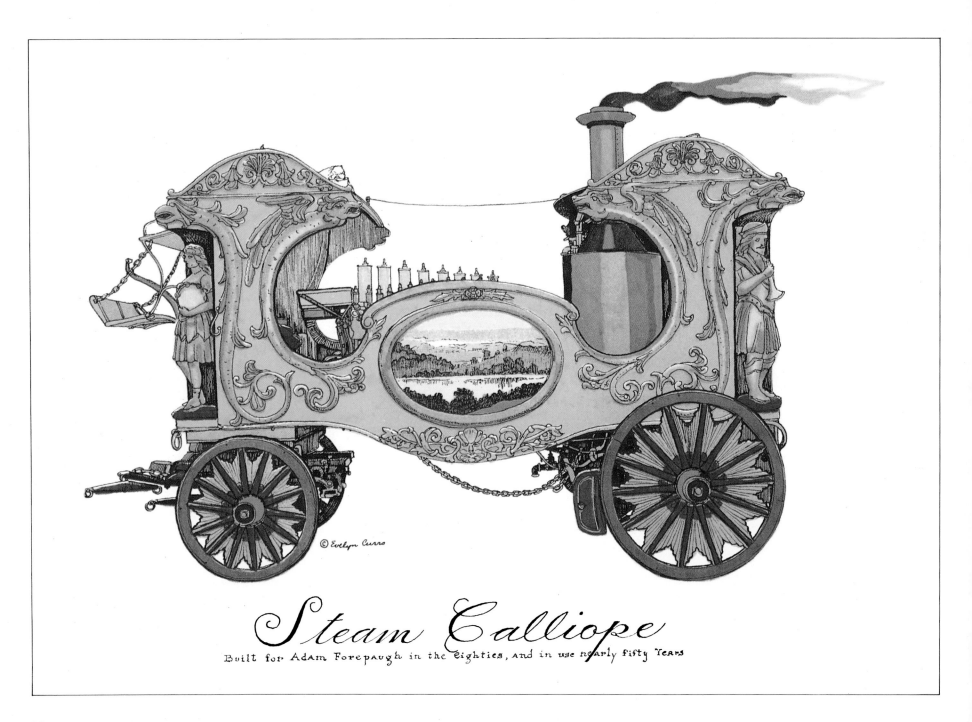

© Evelyn Curro

## Steam Calliope
Built for Adam Forepaugh in the eighties, and in use nearly fifty years

# History and Origins

In the 1640s, when the French actor and dramatist Molière was traveling with a theater company called "l'Illustre Théâtre", performances were held in village barns, or on the occasion of a city fair, on a stage hastily erected between medicine men's booths and the stalls of merchants who sold anything from silks to crafts.

The company was so poor that it could not afford even the cost of a printed bill to advertise its performance. However, the company actors knew how to make the population aware of their presence. It was traditionally called *l'entrée en ville*, but also came to be known by a variety of other names.

For this combination of advertisement and announcement, male performers put on their most colorful costumes, the ladies their most attractive dresses, and the comic applied his most striking makeup and funny attire. At noon the entire company would make its triumphal entrance into the village to the great delight of the local populace. The principal actor, with a deep, strong voice, would herald the performance with resounding cries of "Hear ye! Hear ye!"

*L'entrée en ville* was remarkably effective advertising and didn't cost a *sou*. It had been successful for centuries and was, in fact, the origin of the circus parade.

*Circus World Museum volunteers clean the dust from Cole Bros. Circus'* Asia Wagon *(1902) before it joins the parade.*

Circus companies of the 18th and 19th centuries relied on making this entrance into town for the success of their shows. In Europe, they often hired local cavalry regiment bands to march ahead of the performers. Because the circus was mainly an equestrian art at that time, cavalry officers showed great interest in circus performances and were always ready and willing to cooperate.

In America in 1797, Philip Lailson's equestrians was the first recorded troupe to parade; but whether it was called a pageant in England or cavalcade in France or parade in America, it became a traditional feature of the circus world.

The first true circus parade is considered to be that staged by Philip Astley, whose company did not actually travel. Astley was an equestrian who had established himself near Westminster Bridge in London in 1768, with Astley's Riding School. This became the first circus two years later when he added acrobats, rope dancers, jugglers and clowns to his performance. For this he designed a circular arena, forty-two feet in diameter: the circus ring.

In 1772, one of Astley's pupils, Charles Hughes, opened a similar show near Blackfriar's Bridge, in the vicinity of his former employer's amphitheater. The hot-tempered Astley reacted immediately. "He dressed himself in his blue uniform and rode

*Carvings on the* Asia Wagon *are careful reproductions of the originals, most of which were pilfered before it was rescued in the 1940s.*

his white charger into Westminster, at the head of a procession of two trumpeters, two riders in costume, and a coach where the Little Military Learned Horse sat, helping the clowns to bestow handbills. Here and there, they would halt for Astley to announce feats 'too tedious to mention,' which could be performed only by himself and 'this here company etcetera being in number upwards of fifty, all different' ..." (M. Wilson Disher, *The Greatest Show on Earth*, G. Bell & Sons, Ltd., London, 1937). It was the first circus parade in history. Astley led many others, as did his competitors.

When traveling circuses further established themselves in the 19th century and gained in importance, their parades became more important as well. For major circuses the parade was no longer a simple entry into a city or a cheap, if efficient, way to advertise. It became an event, a procession that was a show in itself. It was free of charge and, of course, it was hoped, an enticement to the bigger event.

In Europe, traveling circuses did not perform in major cities, which had their own resident circus companies housed in circus buildings. But in smaller towns and villages, which didn't have resident entertainers, the visit of a traveling circus was a major event. In fact, the day when an important circus arrived was considered a holiday. Schools and shops were closed to allow everybody to see the circus parade. "Lord" George Sanger's parade was especially popular in England, as was that of the fabulous Louis Soullier, a French equestrian. George Sanger (1826–1911), the English equivalent of P.T. Barnum, began his career as a fairground showman. Upon hearing that Buffalo Bill had been received by Queen Victoria as Colonel Cody, Sanger is reported to have said, "If he is a Colonel, then I am a Lord!" He was known as Lord George Sanger forever after.

Louis Soullier was an extraordinarily effective character. He was married to the widow of Christopher de Bach, owner of the Circus Gymnasticus, the oldest circus in Vienna, Austria. Soullier toured all over Europe and Asia between 1850 and 1866 and even traveled as far as Japan. While in Istanbul, his skills impressed the Sultan Abd Ul Medjid to such an extent that he made the circus equestrian Grand Master of his stables, a distinguished title which came with an array of resplendent medals. These Soullier displayed with great pride while in the ring. From the date of his appointment he wore the costume of his office whenever performing; it was an exotic touch that fitted perfectly his style of showmanship.

When Soullier returned to Europe, he called his circus a "Grand Caravansérail", and his Turkish experience was apparent in every facet of his organization. Other surprises he brought were Chinese and Japanese acrobats and jugglers, never before seen in a circus ring in the Western world.

At no time an ordinary circus, the Grand Caravansérail positions were now even more special, and they needed special titles. Soullier's advance man was a Chargé d'Ambassade and his ringmaster was considered a sort of chamberlain. The circus was given the official title of "Cirque Impérial" and its colorful director was of the opinion that a city should be honored and proud to be visited by it.

The parade, of course, was still a major event in itself, and was widely advertised as such. A handbill of 1854 describes the entry of the Cirque Impérial into the town of Saint Quentin, France. The ceremony (as the parade was described in its advertisements) was scheduled to begin at 2.00 pm; and the first performance of the circus to begin at 7.00 pm.

The parade opened with "*L'Eolienne*, an American carriage so light and so elegant that it was awarded the Gold Medal at the Universal Exhibition of London." Next came the *Chariot de Sainte Cécile*, which was the bandwagon. It was described as a state carriage of a crimson color, with gold ornaments and painted miniatures on the theme of the age of chivalry. It was pulled by four caparisoned horses with "magnificent silver harness". The *Cadrige Impérial* which followed was a stagecoach for "the family of the Director"; it was "richly painted with miniatures, driven 'à la Daumont' with five horses richly harnessed." The aptly-named *La Fortune* was next in the procession; this was the ticket office, driven by the circus accountant. The "young prodigy" (the son of Louis Soullier, who, unfortunately, left the circus and later became a murderer) drove *La Voiture Curricle*, pulled by six black ponies. *La Zéphyrienne* was a charming, light wheeled carriage decorated in red, garnished with Russian leathers, drawn by four dappled horses.

These carriages came behind the circus itself, which was transported by no less than the *Equipages Imperiaux*, "with three horses each, driven by the postillions, containing the extensive material of the moving circus and all the personnel to build it up and tear it down..." This 1854 French handbill is titled "Le Cirque Impérial de Louis Soullier, Ecuyer privilégié de S.M. L'Empereur de Turquie et décoré de l'Ordre Impérial du Nicham-Ifthiar."

The same 1854 handbill specifies that the carriages and wagons were built by Mr. Andrews, Southampton; Mr. Felton, London; Mr. Perry, Bristol; Mr. Nedmann, Bath; Mr. W. Rodgers, Philadelphia (who probably built the "American carriage"); and Mr. Batiste, of Paris. The harnesses ( in silver, bronze and steel) were made by Mr. Frillingham in London. The costumes and dresses were the work of Mr. Moreau, in Paris.

However grandly the handbills described it, the procession was still much a traditional entry into town. With the exception of the bandwagon, if the circus wagons were decorated, they were certainly not yet parade wagons built especially for parade purposes.

Nevertheless, the description of the carriages and the procession were intended to create a sense of luxury and wealth which would ensure the public did not confuse the Cirque Impérial with any of the lesser gypsy shows or carnivals. Soullier's circus was a

*Because of their flamboyance, making circus wagon wheels developed into a special art. Top: The* Orchestmelochor Wagon *wheel is heavily built for use on train-transported circuses. Bottom: Wheel of the* Star Tableau Wagon, *from an earlier period, is lighter and higher for use on circuses that traveled overland.*

*This magnificent wheel adorns the* America Steam Calliope, *a nine-ton wagon that was first a telescoping tableau wagon belonging to the Barnum & Bailey Circus of 1903.*

serious and respectable affair and had to demonstrate the fact at first sight. The band, the glittering bandwagon, and the presence of the "young prodigy" were all part of the actual circus show to come, while the rest of the *entrée* was made up of wagons which served as vehicles for transporting the show. In later years, parades themselves became direct adjuncts to circus performances rather than simply the conveyances of circus companies into town. This was because it was no longer necessary to establish the respectability of the circus as an institution, particularly if the circus in question was a large one. Smaller shows often assumed that this mantle of respectability was theirs as well, sometimes quite incorrectly.

In England, that other great circus character, Lord George Sanger, developed his circus parade in a way that was adopted by American circuses. It has been claimed that nobody ever matched Sanger's parades in luxury. This may not be true, as the great street pageants staged by Adam Forepaugh, Barnum & Bailey and the Ringling Bros. assumed incredible proportions during the golden age of the American circus (roughly from 1870 to 1920). But until then, Sanger was certainly unchallenged. One should remember that when P.T. Barnum opened the Great Roman Hippodrome on Fourth Avenue and 25th Street in New York (later the site of the first Madison Square Garden), he purchased the production ideas, costumes, floats and harnesses of Sanger's Congress of Monarchs which the English showman had earlier produced in London's Agricultural Hall. Barnum democratized it and presented it in 1874 as The Congress of Nations. Clearly, he knew the spectacular when he saw it. However, no one was able to surpass the craftsmanship, finesse and aristocratic beauty of Sanger's circus wagons. Four examples from Sanger's circus are testament to their glory; they are now in the Circus World Museum collection, some of which participate in the Milwaukee Circus Parade. Compared to the primitive folk art of many American wagons (even on such masterpieces as the *Lion and Mirror Bandwagon*, or the *Swan Bandwagon*), the woodcarving and elaborate ornamentation on Sanger's wagons remain unequaled.

Through a description of Sanger's parade in England in the 1880s we can imagine its effect on the population of a small English country town. The parade began with the *Mirrored Tableau*, "a wagon that weighed ten tons, adorned with carved and gilded woodwork and many mirrors," drawn by thirty cream horses. On the *Britannia Tableau*, a telescoping wagon three tiers high, Mrs. George Sanger sat like "Britannia on a penny, a shield with a Union Jack painted on it in her left hand and a gilded trident in her right. A Greek helmet crowned her head. Crouched at her feet was Nero, the lion, and a lamb..." (Nero was sometimes reluctant to participate in these expositions of docility, and Mrs. Sanger, a big cat trainer by profession, was obliged to discard Britannia's dignity on occasion in favor of enforcing the peace — much to the delight of the crowds.)

*Detail of a door of the* Royal Mail Coach, *from Sir Robert Fossett's Circus, England* (circa 1850).

Next came a string of camels, a "herd" of elephants, and 300 riders, artistes and crew-members "dressed up as historical characters". These were followed by the bandwagon: "...angels, sirens, Neptune and mermaids disported on its sides among foamy seas and palm fringed coral reefs; the gilt of the chariot glittered and dazzled in the sun, and the bandsmen...looked resplendent in uniforms of white and gold." This wagon was drawn by a 40-horse hitch.

Finally came the menagerie, in a seemingly endless procession of caged wagons, between which grooms led the larger animals — zebras, camels, llamas and an ostrich. Contrary to American custom, the sides of these wagons were "artfully closed so the onlookers could only surmise what was inside." In fact, Lord George, who in many respects could match his talents at humbuggery with those of P.T. Barnum, had good reason to keep many of his cages shuttered. They were empty!

In 1860, Sanger's strong feeling for pageantry on a grandiose scale led him not only to transform the old entry into town into a staged and spectacular circus parade, but to make the first attempts at a three-ring circus performance and to develop the "spec", which eventually was to become an indoor parade. Because Barnum emulated him, Sanger is considered the grandfather of the purely American circus extravaganza.

In Europe, however, the circus parade remained a British phenomenon. And until the Second World War, countries in Continental Europe continued to stage circuses in permanent circus buildings, active in every city of importance (in the 1920s, Parisians were able to choose between five of them!). So, again, the circus parade was not as strong a tradition, but of course there were exceptions. When the English circus Pinder settled in France at the end of the 19th century, it brought with it the tradition of the circus parade according to Sanger's precedent. It was so successful that the circus kept the tradition alive until the 1950s. Therefore to the French the circus parade was considered a Pinder trademark. From time to time traveling circuses staged small parades as a way of advertising their shows, but they were by no means comparable to American street parades.

When the Barnum & Bailey Circus and Buffalo Bill's Wild West Show went to Europe at the turn of the century, the producers of Continental circuses became aware of the special appeal of the street parade as it had developed in the New World. Shortly thereafter, the combined circus and menagerie blossomed in Europe, and circuses such as Krone, Gleich and Sarrasani, in Germany, staged street parades, although not on a regular basis. While these were major shows, their parades never reached the magnificence of their American counterparts.

# The American Circus Parade

The circus was introduced to the New World in 1793 by the British equestrian John Bill Ricketts. Two years later, his first and only competition arrived in the person of the Swedish equestrian Philip Lailson. When performing in Philadelphia in 1797, Lailson advertised his circus by parading daily through the main streets of the city. It was a simple cavalcade of performers on horseback; since the company was only composed of ten individuals, it was not very impressive, at least by today's standards. Nonetheless, parade watchers could have a free glimpse of the promising charms of Miss Vanice, the leading lady, and feel the desperate need (created by Miss Vanice's brief passing) to attend the circus and witness, with their jaws agape, her feats of horsemanship.

Lailson's example was soon to be followed by his successors as the competition from other forms of entertainment demanded more efficient advertisement than simple handbills and newspaper announcements. In June 1875, an anonymous spectator recalled in the *New York Clipper* the parade of Pépin and Barnet, as it appeared in Cincinatti in April 1824:

> The company paraded every forenoon, preceded by a trumpeter on horseback who, upon reaching the corner of a street, would give blasts upon his instrument which were continued until the foremost horseman in the procession came abreast of him. He would then take a salaam, wheel his horse and gallop him to the next corner, where the same formality would be repeated. Monsieur Pépin, who rode at the head of the performers . . . wore drab breeches top boots and a green tunic with cap and feather to match. . . The Equestrians were attired in tights, black velvet tunics and caps with an ostrich feather in the latter. . . The horses were of the best and groomed to highest grade of skill.

The trumpeter also announced the beginning of the performance in the circus ring. His instrument was then what the whistle is to the modern circus ringmaster.

By 1825 circuses had begun to travel under canvas. The American population was highly mobile, and showmen followed it. They needed horse-drawn wagons not only to transport their equipment but, as the menagerie was soon to become consolidated with the circus, horse-drawn cage wagons as well.

As they had been in Europe, early circus parades in America were a grand entry into town. But American circus managers were compelled to deal with the American public's love of colorful pageantry, and they soon began staging them as a separate show, which

*Left and above: Artistic license gave these charging tigers five claws (tigers have been only four). Parade supporters and invited guests considers it an honor to participate in the rail trek from Baraboo to Milwaukee.*

*Advertising on the circus train cars clearly denotes the pride taken in the circus parade by the state of Wisconsin.*

*Detail from the* America Steam Calliope.

included a cavalcade of circus performers in exotic costumes, a brass band playing patriotic tunes, and a long line of wagons pulled by Percheron teams richly harnessed. But they soon became aware that it was not practical to line up the wagons before entering town, change costumes in a hurry, parade through the main street to the circus lot, change clothes again and set up the tent — all before the performance itself.

As a result, the circus would make an anonymous entry into town, go directly to its lot and build up its tents, and get ready. The circus could then present itself in the best light with a parade to advertise the show. As time went on, wagons became more highly decorated to serve the purpose of the pageant and, eventually, some were especially constructed for parade use only.

Although the purpose of the street parade was to advertise the circus, the parade itself was advertised too. The first known record of a circus parade advertisement is that of Purdy, Welch, Macomber & Co. in 1837. It featured "Royal Golden Chariots, made in London, forty feet high (!) surmounted with revolving tableaux of Golden Elephants, Lions and Tigers" and "Translucent Palaces and Crystal Dens of monstrous Boa Constrictors."

Until the 1870s, circus wagons were drawn from town to town by horses. Practical considerations dictated their size, since they had to be used for both parade purposes and transporting equipment. It became vastly different in 1872, when circuses started to move by rail. The famous American circus motto "bigger and better than ever" was to be fully realized as parade wagons, especially bandwagons, took on gigantic proportions.

It was under this grandiose development that the American circus parade became an institution. It was a free attraction — part of the lure of the circus; in advertisements, it served the same hyperbolic attentions that the performance itself enjoyed; it was organized and staged according to a specific protocol, divided into sections, often led by a mounted band and nearly always concluded with the powerful sound of the uniquely American steam calliope.

Major circuses competed to have the most magnificent, colorful and massive parade. In 1891, Adam Forepaugh's circus assembled a procession of forty-eight different features divided into four sections, including marching bands, mounted performers, tableau wagons, a procession of Indian chiefs, the *Golden Chariot of Neptune* and the steam calliope. Such parades as Forepaugh's were a mile or more long and had hundreds of participants, both two- and four-footed.

Many authorities attribute the real development of the circus parade in America to the return from England of Seth B. Howes, after his successful seven-year tour, in 1864. However, evidence of its development exists in the records of wagon manufacturers prior to that time.

In the 1850s Seth B. Howes left employment with his older brother Nathan's circus and formed a partnership with Joseph C. Cushing. He created the Howes & Cushing Circus, which he took to London, where it played the Alhambra, as well as before Queen

*The Fifth Wisconsin Volunteer Civil War Fife and Drums Corps evokes the period of early American circus parades.*

*Beautifully beplumed and regally costumed by the Circus World Museum's wardrobe department, circus equestriennes await their turn to enter the street parade.*

Victoria. It was a phenomenal success. Upon the return of the show to the United States, it conveniently adopted the name of Howes' Great European Circus. Also important, it brought back to America several ornately carved, gilded, wooden tableau wagons, the first of their type that America had seen. These were telescoping affairs by virtue of the fact that ornately carved platforms, pedestals and protuberances could be elevated out of the bodies of the wagons themselves to create towering, wedding cake-like structures that rolled down city streets — visions of ornamentation for its own sake reminiscent of a style gone out of control, that might, with some stretch of the imagination, be called "barococo". These were remarkably similar to wagons that exist today in the collection of the Circus World Museum (acquired from Sir Robert Fossett's circus, which bought them from Sanger's circus). Not designed to transport animals or supplies, their only purpose was to attract attention. In a word they were breathtaking. Howes' Great European Circus of 1864 was a triumph.

But prior to Howes' return, back in the 1820s, many animal shows and menageries had been on the road in America, most with relatively plain, unornamented cages that were lightly constructed and rolled on high wheels to facilitate passage over rutted mud roads. Purdy and Welch, in 1837, was one of the first of American traveling shows to travel with a parade.

In 1845, Van Amburgh's *Triumphal Car* rode down Broadway, in New York City. It was a bandwagon, twenty feet long, seventeen feet tall, and the first known of American telescoping wagons, although only its small canopy, surmounted by a carved eagle and supported by carved dolphins, could be lowered.

The appearance of exotic wagons such as Van Amburgh's *Triumphal Car* struck the populace of the time with nothing less than awe. Dazzled by their beauty, as well as the colorful glamor of the processions in which they were included, spectators willingly followed the parade to the Big Show.

Researchers, as much victims of the allure of the circus as anyone else, often saw the development of circus parades merely as attachments to one show or another. But a closer look at the work of the wagon builders themselves provides different evidence of the development of the parade.

The *Armamaxa*, or *Imperial Persian Chariot*, was manufactured by New York carriage builder Joseph Stephenson for the Welch, Delevan and Nathan National Circus in 1846–7, and in 1850, C. C. Quick and Co.'s menagerie exhibited an *Automatodeon*, or mechanical band, mounted on a van drawn by elephants and camels. Not to be outdone, Spalding and Rogers Circus introduced another mechanical band called the *Apollonicon*, which was drawn by a forty-horse hitch. (Spalding and Rogers claimed to be the first to put its show on rails, as well.)

By the mid-1850s, bandwagons and ornamental cages were part and parcel of the American circus scene, but it is significant to note that no genuine, fully telescoping

*The weather is hot and the children are restless. It's been a long wait, but soon it will be all eyes forward as the parade passes by.*

tableau wagon had appeared at the time. Stephenson, primarily a carriage builder, was not as well suited to circus wagon building as was another New York manufacturer by the name of Fielding. By 1856 Fielding had a combination band and advertising wagon built for the Lee Bennett Circus and in 1859 had another wagon with carvings by Thomas Brooks (formerly of Stephenson's), built for the same show.

It was at this point that Howes' Great European circus arrived back on American shores, proudly displaying its telescoping tableau wagons. There followed a burst of circus building activity by the Fielding firm: a chariot for the Alexander Robinson show in 1865, a wagon for Van Amburgh in 1866, and one for the Thompson, Smith and Howes' circus in the same year. In 1867, a bandwagon was built for the J. J. French & Co. Circus, and a performing den was constructed for the Adam Forepaugh Circus. The following year, another bandwagon was manufactured for Van Amburgh; and a long band chariot was created for Lewis B. Lent in 1870. In 1872 no less than 16 cages were built for John O'Brien, a notorious circus owner who reputedly carried more drifters, card sharks and short-change artists than performers on his show, and who benefited from their presence by taking a cut of their profits. In 1873, eight cages were made for Adam Forepaugh (who, incidentally, was John O'Brien's former partner).

From about 1879 to 1881, economic pressures resulted in a great regrouping of circus interests. In 1880, James A. Bailey joined with Barnum and Hutchinson to create the Barnum & London Circus. For this, Fielding produced some of its most stylishly ornate wagons — twelve beautifully proportioned and handsomely carved tableau dens, or cages, one of which still exists and is housed in the Circus World Museum collection.

In the same year Adam Forepaugh, Barnum's main competition, ceased his dealings with the Fielding Company and transferred his orders to the Sebastian Manufacturing Company, a firm that created wagons that were heavier, often larger and more massively flamboyant than those produced by Fielding, and which had a master carver for its wagons, Samuel A. Robb and his studio of superb craftsmen. From the Sebastian company, Barnum & London ordered its famous nursery-rhyme and children's-pony floats — *Old Santa Claus* and *The Old Woman Who Lived In A Shoe* in 1883, and five others between 1886 and 1888.

Still, the insatiable demands of the Barnum & Bailey's circus grew. In 1902, Bailey ordered thirteen large, elaborate vehicles from the Sebastian company to be delivered within ten months. Included among these were the stupendous telescoping tableau wagons depicting the continents of Africa, Asia, America and Europe. More were to come. Certainly the largest (and some say the most magnificent) bandwagon ever constructed, the *Two Hemispheres*, emerged from the Sebastian company, replete with handsome carvings by the Robb Studio, for the 1903 season. The monster carriage was twenty feet long, ten feet, six inches high and eight feet wide. Drawn by a team of forty matched bays, it is considered to be one of the greatest contributions to American circus pageantry ever built. Its side carvings of lions and bears are roughly four times life size. Its front corners are emblazoned with richly carved, gilded eagles with outspread wings, while its back is framed by two gigantic elephants, trunks upraised, which shelter an awesome configuration of gilded scrollwork in the midst of which rests a bas-relief of the globe.

When seen in the early 1970s, the *Two Hemispheres Bandwagon* was exhibited at the privately owned Circus Hall of Fame in Sarasota, Florida. Even standing alone, without a mass of draft horses to pull it, the architectural wonder stunned beholders. Its sides had been painted a base color of red, against which a glittering mass of scrollwork made a brassy, striking contrast. An early photograph from the Beggs collection at the Princeton University library reveals that the great chariot had not always been red, but had apparently, for at least one season, been painted white, to lighten the impression of mass and weight. In that lighter-hued version, the incredible gilded scrollwork seemed to be almost airborne; and, despite the wagon's gargantuan size, it had a sense of delicacy, proportion and refinement not frequently encountered in larger American circus vehicles. The great bandwagon is, at this writing, owned by circus model builder John Zweifel.

The demand for thirteen wagons for the 1903 season exhausted woodcarvers in the Robb carving atelier and manufacturers at the Sebastian plant. They had also received an order from the Pawnee Bill Wild West Show for an elaborate Japanese tableau wagon and an equally massive bandwagon. These, together with the thirteen wagon series created for Barnum & Bailey, were the last wagons to come from the Sebastian company. The death of James A. Bailey in 1906 was followed by the purchase of the Barnum & Bailey circus by the Ringling brothers a year later. Trucks began replacing horse-drawn vehicles, and the Sebastian firm closed for business in 1920.

These events signaled the end of an era. Bode, of Cincinnati, Ohio, received its last order (for motorized circus trucks) in 1917. Corwin and Henry Moeller, Jr., of Baraboo, Wisconsin, called it quits as well. For some forty years the Moeller firm had made wagons for every noteworthy circus in the United States including what has come to be known as "the queen of bandwagons", the *Swan Bandwagon*. Henry Moeller and his sons Henry Jr. and Corwin were first cousins to the Ringlings and the Gollmars, who operated another circus based in Wisconsin. True folk artists and superb artisans, the Moellers could not even read a blueprint, a fact that makes many of their superb creations even more miraculous. When both the Ringling and the Gollmar shows moved from Baraboo, the firm faltered, then closed. Although circus wagons continued to be built as late as the 1920s by such manufacturers as those attached to the American Circus Corporation in Peru, Indiana (and some were stylistically charming), the glory days of the gigantic circus street pageants were over.

*Staking their claim, many parade viewers spend the night before the event sleeping on Milwaukee's sidewalks.*

# The Parade Marches into History

As magnificent as they were, circus parades had become expensive ventures. As most American shows were one-day affairs (not easy on the artists, especially if they performed twice daily), performers did not enjoy the tradition of the circus parades as much as the public. Even Barnum & Bailey had tried to discontinue its street parade as early as 1905. But it was resumed the following year, after the management realized that it was still the best possible gatherer of crowds.

Following the First World War, mounting a circus parade became increasingly difficult. Cities had grown and circuses were forced to find lots far from the center of town, making parade routes longer — to the great displeasure of the performers. Smiling under the broiling sun atop a glittering wagon or on a caparisoned horse with two performances ahead of them on a longer, more tiring parade route, was no joy. Understandably, they dreamed of doing away with street parades. The same was true of grooms and other circus workers who took part in the gigantic spectacles. Almost nobody who took part in them liked them.

The economic climate had changed as well. What was expensive at the turn of the century was doubly so twenty years later. City streets were being paved with asphalt, and city planners didn't relish the idea of huge wagon wheels tearing them up on a hot summer day. With both the advent of the motor car and paved roads, traffic was a new problem, and circus parades complicated it further.

Under such pressures, the joy and magic of the circus parade was doomed. In 1921, Ringling threw in the towel, and the giant, amazing, colorful, eyecatching, dazzling circus parade vanished. Smaller shows still carried a shortened version of the once glorious tradition through the 1930s; but these, too, faded slowly in the 1940s.

Elements of the street parade, suggestions of it, remained in the "specs" of the largest American circuses. But the excitement of circus magic brought directly into our everyday environment, the street, has long gone, as has the wheezing of the steam calliope.

Certainly among the reasons why the street parade disappeared was the fact that it had, in many cases, exceeded the very attraction that it was supposed to advertise. It became an event unto itself and was, furthermore, free. Among the hundreds of thousands entertained and amazed by street parades, comparatively few could get in to witness actual performances. Even if they did so, how could a few jugglers, animal trainers, trapeze artists, equestrians or clowns hope to create a more vivid impression upon generally unsophisticated audiences than the seemingly endless file of exotic wagons that

*Like an exotic serpent, the circus train glides slowly through the countryside on its way to the big event. Note the headless dragon on the* Golden Age of Chivalry Tableau Wagon; *double heads and tail are safely stored inside.*

*Perfectly reflecting the day's euphoria, this clown flap-foots her way along the four-mile parade route . . .*

mesmerized townfolk with their size and razzle-dazzle allure? It is reasonably safe to assume that the huge sums expended on the creation and mounting of elaborate street processions must have come perilously close to out-distancing the amounts taken in at the box office, income from huckstering at the "front end" notwithstanding. In short, the circus seems to have become an appendage to its own street parade.

There was another economic consideration. Many cities would not, or could not, accommodate the wholesale stoppage of other commerce created by the massive intrusion of circus parades, no matter how grand, glorious, or exciting they might have been. In many localities all local commerce simply ground to a halt on the day the circus came to town; and this was aggravated by the fact that many circuses, which lured local citizens into the outlying areas for the afternoon or evening, had compounded the economic ill by taking over and tying up the main street shopping area with their parades in the morning as well.

In the days when circus parades were at their most extensive, their participation in the economic life of cities and towns, such as the purchase of supplies and food for people and animals, was not readily perceived. In the popular mind, the circus was made up of "foreigners" who came to town, took the money and ran. This undercurrent of opinion, enhanced by periodic visits of genuinely dishonest circus operations, persisted regardless of the popularity of free street parades. So it may be said that, in a sense, the circus street parade bowed to economic pressures from both within and without. It passed into history when the social climate dictated.

But it is living history. Just prior to Milwaukee's Great Circus Parade of 1985, 94-year-old Merle Evans, Bandmaster for Ringling Bros. Circus for fifty years and himself a participant in some of the original circus parades even before that, looked up and down the long line of circus wagons, assembled costumed riders and exotic beasts: "This is the biggest, grandest circus parade that's ever been put on anywhere," he said. "Of that I'm sure!"

# The Circus World Museum and Its Early Street Parades

*. . .while this hobo chooses to rest his suspiciously well-booted feet before beginning to march.*

It all started back in 1954, when a gentleman by the name of John M. Kelly took the legal steps to incorporate the Circus World Museum in Baraboo, Wisconsin. On June 24th of that year Kelly, who had been an attorney for the Ringling Bros. for over thirty years, joined forces with Fred C. Gollmar, one of the founders of Gollmar Bros. Circus and cousin to the Ringlings, and Fred's son, Judge Robert Gollmar. The three signed the original incorporation papers.

As incorporated, the Circus World Museum is owned by the State Historical Society of Wisconsin. The purpose of the museum is to collect and preserve circus history on a worldwide basis and to make it available to the public.

But why a circus museum in Wisconsin? The answer lies with two circus owners from Brewster, New York called the Mabie brothers. In 1847 they took their show into the fast developing Midwest, in part because the East was so overstocked with circuses. With a burgeoning population in Wisconsin, their season was successful, and rather than head east to winter quarters, they purchased land in the village of Delavan, Wisconsin. It was Wisconsin's first circus — a year before it became a state in the Union. From 1840 to 1850, the area saw a population increase of 30,000 to 300,000. The market was there, industry was blossoming, horses were in good supply; and, most important, the supply of hay and grains for horses and menagerie animals was excellent. The Mabies settled down, at least as much as any circus family can settle down.

Their presence in Wisconsin acted as a draw for others in the circus profession. Sometimes performers left a show to start one of their own, so that within fifty years, Delavan was the seat of twenty-six different circuses. Living became so crowded that some performers and prospective circus owners moved to other Wisconsin towns, where they established themselves. This influenced local residents, many of whom wanted to try their hand at the profession. Thus Wisconsin became a thriving center of the circus arts. According to local historians, there were approximately one hundred circus titles in twenty-seven Wisconsin cities and towns. Like most lists of circus statistics, this may represent an inflated number of actual circuses; but the circus activity in Wisconsin was nonetheless notable, and it included some genuine heavyweights in the profession, names like W. C. Coup, the Ringlings, Gollmars, Lindemans and Robbins.

The move of the Mabie brothers (together with their experienced managerial talent) from Brewster, New York (which until then had been what is called the "Cradle of the American Circus") to Delavan, Wisconsin, created such an influx of talent that Wisconsin

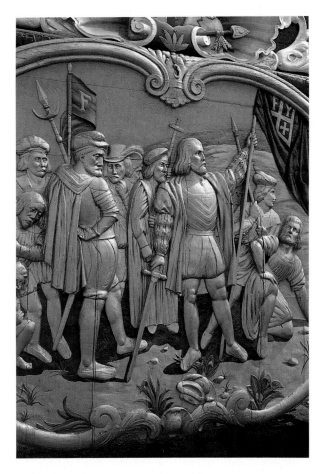

*Columbus discovers America. This is one of the two bas-relief panels that adorn the* Pawnee Bill Wild West Show Bandwagon, *built in 1903.*

was soon called the "Mother of Circuses" — and it was said that in moving, the "Mother of Circuses" had snatched her baby from the "Cradle of the Circus"!

It is appropriate that the Circus World Museum is a National Historic Landmark. Like any good museum, it is more an active center than a mere depository (although it is the world's greatest depository of circus-related articles and information). It is also the site of the original winter quarters of the Ringling Bros. Circus, which had become the largest and most renowned circus in the world and had developed into the most extensive circus empire that ever existed.

Among the several directors of the museum is one to whom particular credit should be given as a leader and coordinator (his fame as circus author has tended to draw attention away from his museum work). That person is Charles Philip Fox, known to circus fans as "Chappie". It was he who spotlighted the collection of historic circus wagons as of prime importance to the museum; and, with an innate sense of its value, it was Fox who came up with the idea to launch a parade of beautifully restored tableau dens and bandwagons down Main Street. It was a visionary master stroke and precisely the shot of adrenalin that the struggling museum needed.

Here is a brief synopsis of the Fox years at the Circus World Museum, told, appropriately, by Chappie himself.

"By the time the Circus World Museum opened its doors for the first time on July 1, 1959, the horse-drawn circus parade was an event of the distant past. A few of the grand, old parade wagons were collected and put on display at the Baraboo, Wisconsin, Museum.

On January 2, 1960, I took over the directorship of the Circus World Museum. In my opinion, it was important to acquire as many circus wagons (both parade and baggage) as possible simply because it was the presence of these vehicles that made the traveling circus an unusual enterprise — almost unique.

So we set our sights on the collection of circus wagons, feeling that the myriad of circus buffs would appreciate these displays. The public would also enjoy the feeling of nostalgia seeing these wagons fully restored. It was an effort that paid off.

In 1953, I had the pleasure of having published a photo history of the old street parades. In the many years of research while preparing this work for publication, I built quite a file of where these old circus parade wagons were located around the country; so with this list as a starting point, the letters, phone calls and personal visits began. One of my favorite aphorisms is 'You can't plow a field by turning it over in your mind — do it now!' I must say that believing in this maxim was a key to the success of developing the museum's wagon collection which today numbers around one hundred and fifty historic vehicles.

The wagons began to roll into Baraboo on flatcars and lowboy trailer trucks; and by 1962, the collection was beginning to take shape.

One summer day, I was cutting up jackpots with circus model builder John Zweifel. We were dreaming of the future of the Circus World Museum; the conversation came around to the wagons — then to circus parades. That was the flux needed to promote the idea of an old fashioned circus street parade.

Such a parade would do two things. It would present circus history in a flashy, animated way, and it would advertise and promote the museum.

I got in touch with twelve top executives of major Wisconsin corporations looking for a sponsor, and was politely turned down. My next contact was to be the Jos. Schlitz Brewing Company. I was advised to see Mr. Ben Barkin, the head of one of Milwaukee's top public relations firms. Schlitz was one of his accounts.

In the fall of 1962, at our first meeting, I could tell by the excitement in Mr. Barkin's eyes that he grasped the significance of the circus parade. He sensed its color, its excitement, its uniqueness, and above all the fact that it was an event perfectly suited for the entertainment of an entire family.

In those early days, the Circus World Museum was as poor as the proverbial church mouse. As a result, my presentation amounted to little more than a handful of old parade photos and my verbal explanations; but it worked. Ben Barkin's imagination carried the day. When we went to see Mr. Bob Uihlein, Chairman of the Board and President of the Jos. Schlitz Brewing Company, it took only twenty minutes to sell the idea. Mr. Uihlein turned to Ben and said, 'Let's go for it, Ben.'

On July 4, 1963, the first Schlitz Circus Parade marched down the streets of Milwaukee.

There were those who said. 'How can something as archaic as a circus parade be revived?' Well, they were wrong in that attitude. For the next eleven years, parade attendance on the city streets soared. During the late 1960s and early 1970s, the crowds numbered around 800,000; and in the same period, attendance at the Circus World Museum jumped to an all-time high.

Each year, Mr. Uihlein and the people at the Schlitz Brewing Company asked, 'What will be new for the next year?' That attitude enabled the Circus World Museum to go after circus wagons that had previously been beyond the realm of possibility to acquire. Example: The glorious English parade wagons given to the museum by the Sir Robert Fossett Circus of Northampton, England, had their transportation costs underwritten by the Schlitz Brewing Company. Today, these wagons are among the most magnificent in the parade.

Example: Louis Goebel gave the museum a large group of beautiful wagons from the Hagenbeck-Wallace circus, but they were located in Thousand Oaks, California; Schlitz paid for transporting them to Baraboo and for their restoration.

So it was that the Great Circus Parade grew in size and in scope.

In October of 1972, I had left the Circus World Museum to accept a position with Ringling Bros. and Barnum & Bailey Circus. Late in 1973, the Schlitz Company announced that they would give up the sponsorship of the circus parade, and no effort was made to locate another sponsor.

There followed a continual stream of telephone calls, letters, requests and appeals for the return of the parade. Luckily they didn't fall on deaf ears. Ben Barkin again rose to the occasion and responded to the clamor by raising $750,000 to fund a revival of the great event — the enormously successful Great Circus Parade that took place in Milwaukee on July 14, 1985. Again, there were doubters. 'The bloom is off. The excitement is gone,' they protested. Again they were wrong. After a twelve-year hiatus, the Great Circus Parade, with Bob Parkinson as parade coordinator, was a huge success."

*Blare and oompah are circus parade stock in trade.*

Along with the host of enthusiasts who have witnessed the circus parade in Baraboo, Milwaukee, and Chicago, Chappie regards this traveling show from the Circus World Museum to be a genuine national treasure. So, too, is the museum itself, where the priceless collection of more than one hundred and sixty wagons is just a small part of the whole collection. Its library and research center holdings far eclipse circus collections anywhere else in the world. Nearly 7,000 circus posters, 20,000 black-and-white negatives, 50,000 black-and-white photoprints, over 1,000 programs, 12,000 newspaper advertisements dated from 1793 to the present, 5,850 band music portfolios and manuscripts including the Merle Evans Music Library, trade journals and newspapers, circus authorities, papers and collections, Ringling Bros. Circus ledgers from 1897 through 1917, as well as the show's archives from 1919 through 1967, Gollmar Bros. Circus ledgers from 1891 through 1916. The list reads on until the serious student of the circus begins to feel as wide-eyed as a child who experiences his first circus performance!

In 1985, new impetus for the museum's development came when Greg Parkinson was appointed as acting director. The response among circus fans nationwide was joyous. At 34, too young to have experienced the grand old era of street parades himself, Parkinson nevertheless made his way up through the ranks at the museum, where he had worked for seven years, and where he had been Program and Endowment Director since 1982. His expertise and energy suits perfectly the upbeat nature of museum activities and his vision for the museum will continue to keep it the best of its kind.

Parkinson himself says, "The direction in which we must move in the coming years has to be toward greater fulfillment of our mission to collect, preserve and present circus history. We have to build a progressive Circus World Museum with a national reputation for greatness."

# The Big Weekend

*Too young to remember the heyday of circus, these high schoolers are new participants in a tradition that they will probably never forget.*

There is a sound which perhaps more than any other is reminiscent of the circus parade and which marked its revival in Milwaukee. It is a resounding "clonk".

And it is referred to by more than one historian describing the noise from the great wagons of oak, hickory or maple as they trundled along the street. It comes from elaborate wagon wheels bumping against shoulders of wooden axles, and it is deeper than sounds created by other wagon wheels because these are more massive and are often adorned with fancy webs of wood between their spokes.

Although parade watchers hear every sound typical to a street parade — the grinding of metal rimmed wheels against pavements; the clop of hundreds upon hundreds of hooves as impatient horses slowly draw magnificent chariots around corners and along broad city streets; the soft padding of the elephants' shuffle-step; and the raucous blaze and oompah of one circus band after another — they don't understand until they hear that sound. Even the dulcet pipings of air calliopes that contrast markedly with the shrieks of the great steam calliope at parade's end could not say "circus" more than that "clonk".

Milwaukee had last seen a recreation of old time circus parades in 1973, when the Jos. Schlitz Brewing Company had sponsored the gala event. Chappie Fox was the guiding light of the parades back then, and he was consultant during the 1985 parade as well, making notes on a little pad and peering at the proceedings from beneath his felt hat, a Fox trademark. Robert Parkinson was parade chairman that year and worked closely with his son Greg, newly appointed director of Baraboo's Circus World Museum. The event was more than usually special because Milwaukee had not seen a circus parade for twelve years.

Alongside Jackson Street in the shadow of Milwaukee's elevated Lake Drive exists an enormous vacant lot, once used by Ringling Bros. and Barnum & Bailey Circus when it toured under canvas. But, as on every circus parade weekend since July 11th and 12th 1985, it was crammed with exotically shaped and carved wagons of every description that had been unloaded from the Museum's circus train in the old way, with the use of winches, ropes and horse teams — a spectacle in itself. Seventy-five of these historic circus vehicles joined the Carson & Barnes Circus, the largest still performing under canvas, together with the circus train locomotive and several gaudily painted freight cars. (The Carson & Barnes Five Ring Circus was featured during the days preceding the Parade in 1985 and 1986. Other circuses have been featured since.) The circus had erected its great, red and white striped tent not far from where its elephants had been staked outside in a picket line. There were twenty-four of them, to which had been added

*This immaculately made-up clown seems to be having as good a time as she is giving.*

Tony Diano's Big Tommy, the largest tusker on the road, and his four female companions, and three elephants owned by Buckles Woodcock. Big Tommy has since become famous as Ringling Bros. and Barnum & Bailey Circus' star elephant, King Tusk.

Also included yearly is a full menagerie display and the visiting circus' contingent of performing horses. Many red, white and silver trailers are on hand as well. All of this blends into a scene that assumes surrealistic qualities, like a giant, three-dimensional kaleidoscope.

Backed by the somewhat sterile, modern Milwaukee skyline, the huge, dusty lot with all its circus paraphernalia glitters like a many-faceted jewel in the heat. Lining its border on one side is a phalanx of large striped tents, shelter for many of the horses that are assembled to pull the circus wagons through Milwaukee's streets.

In the parade revival of 1985, crowds of ticket holders mingled with circus fans who were content merely to soak up the atmosphere in front of the huge circus tent. Many friends from widely separated areas of the country were surprised to run into each other in the crowd. The muffled sounds of a lively circus band added to the excitement as performances took place under the big top. Between performances, the South Shore Concert Circus Band from East Bridgewater, Massachusetts, set up chairs in front of the circus tent and entertained visitors outside.

The backyard and adjoining streets are a beehive of activity for the staff, not just onlookers; here the Circus World Museum officials and staff execute a dry run of horse teams (numbering from two to forty horses each) hitched to the elaborate wagons that they will draw through downtown Milwaukee on "Parade Sunday." This is the first time that most of the teams and drivers will see the wagon that they have been delegated to pull. Among drivers, it is considered an honor to participate in the parade. Many compete for the privilege and note publication of "their" wagons and team's photos in the local press with special pride.

There are horses everywhere: in addition to those used for hauling the great wagons, there are horses used by the circus for bareback, liberty and dressage performances, and large numbers of horses used by riding clubs that will be decked out in circus finery for the parade. They come from so many states, as well as Canada, that one onlooker viewing a smaller parade held in 1985 at the same time in St. Thomas, Ontario, asked a local resident why so many vehicles were pulled by oxen. "The horses are probably all down in Milwaukee," was the answer.

That year as the sunshine turned to dusk on Saturday, a muggy haze settled over the circus lot and parade staging area. In the darkness came the periodic clanking of hardware as harnesses were set out to be fitted onto hundreds of horses in the morning. The long, grey picket line of elephants weaved, shadowy and silently, in the dark. A few words of Spanish were exchanged by circus performers lounging in the front of their trailers; and a

Top: *Clowns pose for a group portrait before entering the line of march.*

Bottom: *The endless waiting is nearly over as the boom of the bass drum can be heard in the distance.*

bubbly "whuff" emerged from "Miss Oklahoma", the circus hippopotamus, as she settled into her tank for the night.

Somewhere a tiger moaned before drifting off to sleep, and the eerie half light from tents, trailers and floodlights on the circus grounds fell on the macabre silhouettes of century-old carvings, some of which had traveled the world to arrive in Milwaukee for this very special celebration on a very special day.

Parade Day — Sunday, July 14, 1985 — was much like its predecessor — uncomfortably warm and muggy. Official temperature at parade time was 84°, and relative humidity at 74 percent. Temperature and humidity combined to produce a dangerous heat-stress index of 90 to 95 over most of the parade route, although occasional breezes from Lake Michigan cooled spectators. Persons who were exposed to full sunshine risked heat-stress index readings of 100 to 105.

In spite of these enervating conditions, only an estimated 65 persons were treated for heat exhaustion by Red Cross first aid stations that day, although 330 were treated for injuries related to heat. The paved surface of the parade route reached 115°, according to a *Milwaukee Sentinel* reporter. As the day progressed, the temperature climbed to 87°, prohibiting visitors from gaining much relief when they reported to Red Cross first aid tents; the temperature inside was 85°!

And the parade itself was not without unexpected excitement. At its start, cage wagon number 83, once a star of Barnum & Bailey's parades in 1910, was divested of four of its six-horse hitch after the misbehaving quartet crashed into a utility pole and broke free from the wagon. The cage, which carried two zebra colts, halted when two of the horses went around one side of the utility pole and two others went around the other. Spectators scattered as the horses entered the sidewalk area. Some of the reins broke apart, and the center pole to which the forward team was harnessed was broken. A newspaper dispensing box fastened to the utility pole crashed to the ground, and one of the horses galloped north, where it was caught by an alert police sergeant.

The same street corner was nearly the scene of a similar mishap when horses pulling the handsome *Lion and Mirror Bandwagon* started to get out of control. Luckily, the animals were slowed down in time and did not crash into a police barricade that sealed off a portion of the street.

As it does yearly, the police department attempted to anticipate any possible problem. Tow trucks, equipped with special rigging in the event that any of the larger animals suffered from the heat and had to be removed from the parade line-up for treatment, were ready on side streets. The Red Cross was fully prepared as well. (It maintains thirteen aid stations along the parade route, and its volunteers pass out paper cups full of water to exhausted musicians, parade participants and viewers.) At the corner of North 6th and West Wells streets, Red Cross workers sprayed marching paraders and animals

*How about a wave for the passing photographer?*

with water from a fifteen-foot hose attached to a city fire-hydrant, a welcome shower in the sweltering heat.

Although spectators had been encamped along the curbing as early as 6 pm the day before the parade, most of the incidents related to heat occurred on the morning and the afternoon of the parade itself, as visitors' patience began to wear thin.

At about 11:30 am, a lady fell from a walkway along the Milwaukee river into the river itself. Amid much tooting of whistles, emergency squads arrived as draw bridges were lifted to permit access to the woman, who clung valiantly to a cement piling. She was removed to a police launch, which puttered off up the river to the applause of onlookers from the street.

Asked later whether the unfortunate accident was only that, or was instead an attempt at a suicide, a member of Milwaukee's finest appeared shocked and responded, "Suicide? Are you crazy? She would have missed the parade!"

Elsewhere along the route, visitors were surprised to see that the orderly crowds of Milwaukee were restrained to appropriate areas by the mere placement of pink dotted lines along the street. County bus service was free for the day into and out of downtown Milwaukee; and the downtown area was sealed off to those who tried to gain access from the elevated superhighway running through it. It was a day of excitement, full of eager anticipation that spoke well not only of the parade's organizers but of the citizens themselves. It showed Milwaukee at its best.

On Wisconsin Avenue, outside the Pfister Hotel (headquarters and gathering place for parade officials), the East Bridgewater Circus Concert Band, transplanted from its location on the circus lot the day before, serenaded onlookers as parade time drew near. Onlookers sat in chairs set up behind barricades by the hotel management, a convenience that was and still is duplicated by other hotels along the parade route. Serving as prime vantage points, fire escapes became increasingly populated, as did windows above street level and building rooftops everywhere in the vicinity. Merchants who remembered the record crowds of a dozen years earlier taped over store windows at sidewalk level; for there was only a small passageway between the area designated for parade spectators and storefronts through which pedestrians might pass — if they could squeeze through at all.

Almost imperceptibly the tempo of anticipation increased. Murmurs swept through the crowd like breezes through a wheatfield. The mere escape of a helium-filled balloon could cause applause, exaggerated laughter and comment, almost as if it were a planned part of the festivities.

Finally, a great round of applause arose as the movie actor Ernest Borgnine and his wife, Tova, appeared in advance of the parade itself. Attired in a broadly designed clown costume, Borgnine clowned joyously, performing little shuffle steps in time to the band music and greeting children as if they were his own. Ernest and Tova Borgnine have, since this first appearance in 1985, become a traditional presence in Milwaukee on parade day. In the years following, the excitement that precedes the circus section of the parade has remained essentially the same.

A contingent of high-wheeled bicycles careens past, followed by a section filled with antique automobiles. These weave from side to side along the street so that the parade behind could keep up.

Then, with the parade bearing down upon onlookers, the huge crowd seems to fall momentarily silent. There appears a kind of vacuum in the air as people simply stand, jaws agape, staring at the street.

The quiet is pierced by shrill cries of "Here it comes! Here it comes!" as, over a gentle slope in the street, the beautiful *Swan Bandwagon*, drawn by eight Belgian horses, comes into view.

It doesn't matter that two horse-drawn carriages, one signboard wagon, nine mounted flag bearers and a Civil War fife-and-drum corps of the Union Army all precede this queen of circus wagoncraft. It is the great leading bandwagon, with its wheels grinding against the concrete pavement, that is the first example of antique Americana to put an official stamp on the event. As it passes, a pandemonium of sheer joy breaks loose. Old timers weep openly, and children who have probably never seen a wagon larger than their own red American Express carts, shriek with glee, jump up and down, and applaud violently as they watch that extraordinary spectacle. Here is the Great American Circus Parade, come home after years of absence. There wasn't a single spectator who was not aware of the importance and magnitude of the event in 1985, and the feeling persists, year after year, as the grand revival marches on.

And it is no fantasy pageant. It is as real as it is magnificent. The beautiful woodcarvings are original, created by superb craftsmen, and range from the strikingly primitive to the most sophisticated and delicately subtle. The physical effort required to mount the gargantuan production is equally genuine and everywhere apparent.

It is a procession bursting with the energy of sheer happiness, one about which many people will write for months after it passes into history, but few can describe with justice, precisely because it is so visual. It is this grand and glorious banquet that awaits you in this book. Perhaps, as you read, you too can imagine the shivers of excitement caused by the cry that went out as circus parades entered American towns and cities in days gone by:

*Waiting for the parade affords a great chance to catch up on a suntan.*

"HOLD YER HOSSES! THE ELEPHANTS ARE COMING!"

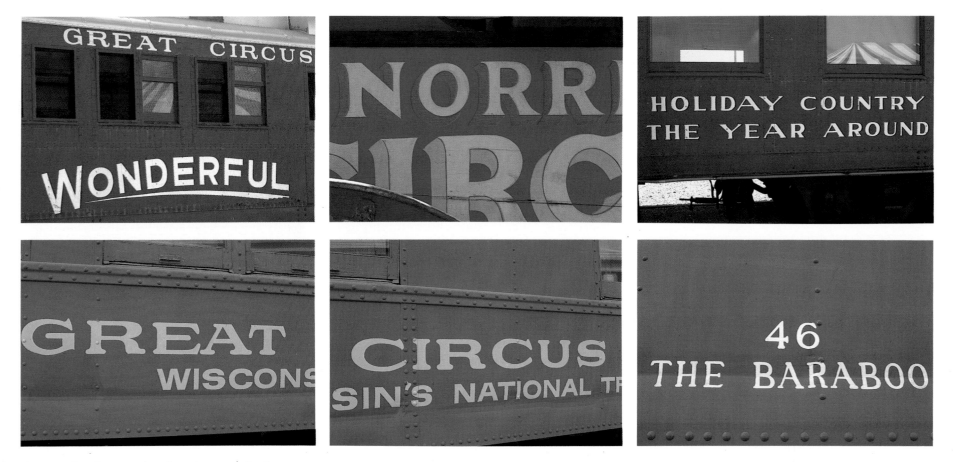

*Cars on the circus train advertise not only the parade but the charms of Wisconsin as well.*

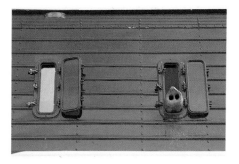

*"This must be Milwaukee," this elephant probably thinks as she tests the breezes with the tip of her trunk.*

*Diesel is replaced by steam for the ceremonial, early evening arrival of the circus train in Milwaukee. Old reliable 1385 is sometimes helped to make the grade by diesels pushing from behind.*

*Despite the disappearance of the circus' traditional arrival in town, the sight of the magical caravan retains its magnetic appeal.*

*The local band, color guard and—of course—photographers are all on hand for 1385's arrival.*

Top: *Flatcars that carry the circus wagons are genuine old circus railroad cars, kept in the collection of the Circus World Museum.*

*A team of Percherons unloads the wagons in the old-time way—a fascinating sight for circus buffs.*

*Young Ryan Enerson's wish to be part of the parade becomes a reality — probably a once-in-a-lifetime event that he will recount for years.*

*Organized by Walter Wilde and Bernie Peck of Milwaukee, a cavalcade of antique automobiles, some carrying dignitaries and celebrities, seemingly transports visitors back to a period when horse-drawn vehicles ruled the roads. This pre-circus section of the parade also includes the United States Navy Band from the Great Lakes Naval Training Center (Illinois), Flag units, Coast Guard Precision Marching Units (Washington, D.C.), motorized trolley cars, an old-time police paddy wagon, Mounted Police patrol, high-wheel bicycles of the 1890s, the Fifth Wisconsin Volunteer Civil War Fife and Drums Corps and a group of horse-drawn carriages.*

To some young people, old auto names may be just names. But the magic of seeing old automobiles combined with the allure of the parade and the festive spirit of the day bridges the generation gap.

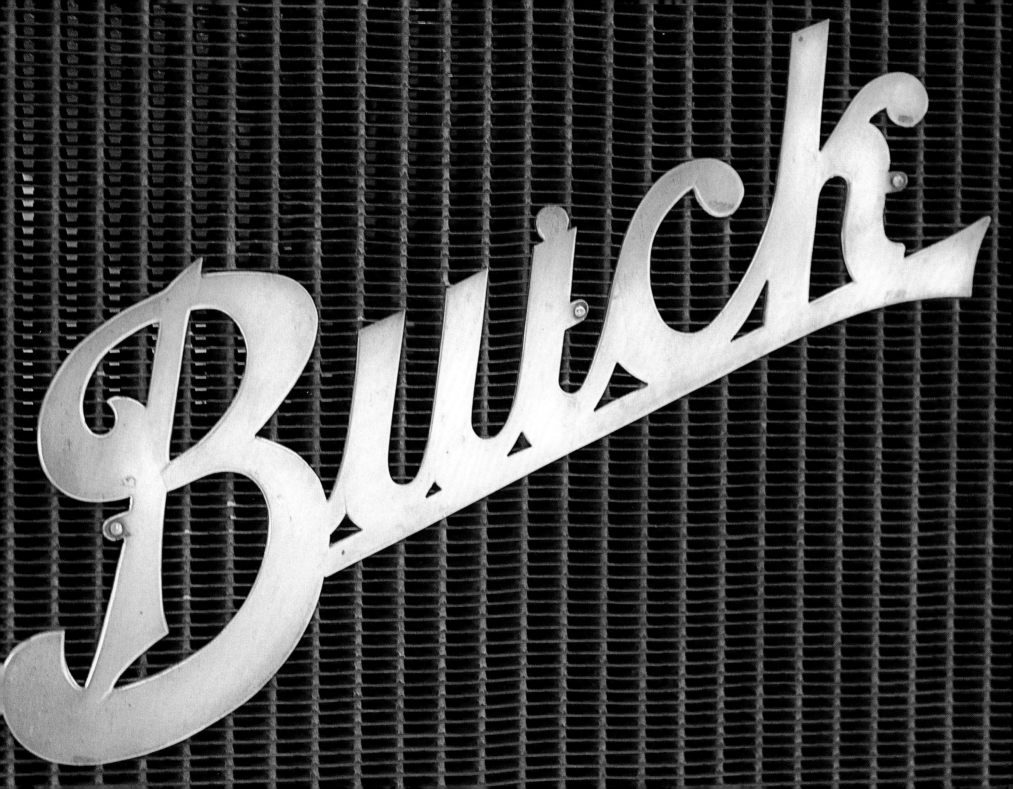

*Massed flags of the fifty United States are displayed by the U.S. Navy Flag Unit as part of the opening of the parade.*

*Classic automobiles add color and nostalgia to the parade event.*

Marching bands, many of them from local high schools, add zip and vibrancy to the long parade. The enormous Baraboo High School Marching Band (top right), entirely costumed as clowns, provides spectacular imagery, filling the streets with music and color.

*The Wild West section of the parade.
Pictured here:*
*The* Concord Stage Coach, *featured in
the Buffalo Bill Wild West Show at the
turn of the century; a covered wagon
of the 101 Ranch Real Wild West
(1926), pulled by a team of oxen; and,
rounding the corner, Adam
Forepaugh's stringer wagon No. 201.
Stringer wagons carried seat sections
for the big top. When empty, they were
often used as moving stages in
parades. This one carries James
Herndon's Dixieland Band of Chicago
and a lively group of dancing,
celebrating clowns.*

*The* Introduction Wagon *opens the parade's main attraction, the circus division.*

*Old-time circus parades made great use of patriotic themes. These mounted flag bearers (center) are reminders of this grand tradition, as are the patriotic ornamentations which adorn panels (top left) and wheels (above) of a section of the parade called "Our Country."*

*Massive crowds fill the grandstands erected by Milwaukee's leading hotels and corporations. Seen here is the Orchestmelochor Wagon, pulled by a six-horse hitch. This four-ton wagon housed a huge band-organ which the Barnum & London Circus billed, back in 1882, as the "Golden Voiced Organ of Vienna." It was later transformed into a baggage wagon and remained in use until the 1920s.*

Top: *Superb ornamentation embellishes the* Temple Tableau Wagon, *a vehicle of undetermined ancestry that came from England, courtesy of Sir Robert Fossett's Circus.*

Above: *This Medusa head decorates the glass-enclosed snake den built by Bode Wagon Works of Cincinnati, Ohio, for Ringling Bros. Circus in 1903.*

Right: *The* Lion and Gladiator Tableau Wagon *No. 102, owned by Ringling Bros. and Barnum & Bailey Circus, is on loan to the Circus World Museum. It is here pulled by an eight-horse hitch.*

The Whiskers Cage Wagon No. 88—so named because of its four, bearded corner figure carvings—is here ridden by Kay Rosaire, the lion trainer, and one of her regal, feline friends.

*The* Whiskers Cage Wagon *is seen here from another angle. Note the outrider, on the left, ready to assist in case of difficulty with the wagon horses, and parade attendants guarding against the public approaching the cage. The lion, incidentally, failed to react to the bandwagon just behind. For a circus lion, it's all in a day's work.*

Right: *"A living leopard loose on the streets!" Well—not really. But at least it's the next best thing, as Darlene Williams waves from England's handsome* Temple Tableau Wagon.

Top two: *The incessant clopping of hooves is one of the sounds characteristic of the Great Circus Parade, just as plumed and caparisoned horses are virtually its visual trademark.*

*The imposing* Twin Lions Telescoping Tableau Wagon *was used originally by "Lord" George Sanger's Circus in England, then by Sir Robert Fossett's Circus, from which it was donated to the Circus World Museum. More than a century old, it stands 17 feet 7 inches high, 14 feet 4 inches long and weighs 7,400 pounds.*

## The Two Hemispheres

World's largest bandwagon, built in New York City in 1896 for Barnum & Bailey's "Greatest Show on Earth".

*Hello from Hollywood! Ernest and Tova Borgnine, together with their make-up artist, Keith Crary, are lively and much loved celebrity clowns in Milwaukee's Great Circus Parade. Their participation has become a tradition.*

Left: *The* Two Hemispheres Bandwagon *was built for the 1903 season of Barnum & Bailey Circus and is said to be the greatest contribution to American circus pageantry ever made. The gigantic vehicle has often been drawn by a forty-horse hitch.*

*Spectators and participants spend much of the parade time socializing with friends.*

Howe's Great London Circus Cage Wagon No. 82 was built in the 1920s.

A high school brass band blasts away at "Barnum & Bailey's Favorite," adding greatly to the festive spirit of the day.

Bobby Moore's Indian and African elephants add a flamboyant splash of spectacle as they parade down Wisconsin Avenue.

Left: The Schlitz Bandwagon was built in 1972 for the "Old Milwaukee Days" parade and stands as the last traditional bandwagon to have been built. Pictured here, aboard the circus train flatcar, its "chocks" have just been removed so it can be unloaded.

Tova Borgnine's costume is a fine example of the elegance and splendor of circus dress.

Sea Shell Tableau Wagon *No. 84 was featured in Ringling Bros. Circus' parades from 1914 to 1918.*

*Terrell Jacobs' Cage Wagon No. 24, a small vehicle pulled by six ponies, displays a lion cub named Clawdine. (Terrell Jacobs was one of America's foremost cat trainers in the 1930s.)*

Left: *This Betsy Ross impersonator is virtually obscured by flags on a float bearing her name. A temporary "No Parking" sign was erected to clear the way for the parade.*

*Ringling Bros. Circus' Snake Den (1906) carries the Humbert family of Lombard, Illinois, and their boa constrictors.*

*St. George and the Dragon*

Built in the late Seventies for the Adam Forepaugh Circus

Built in 1879 for Adam Forepaugh's Circus—a serious rival of Barnum's—and originally called St. George and the Dragon *due to its large telescopic upper structure, this wagon was acquired by* Ringling Bros. Circus in 1890. It was converted into a bandwagon which became known as the Lion and Mirror Bandwagon *and was later used on the Cole Bros. Circus as late as the 1930s. It is seen on* the next page as it appears today in the Great Circus Parade.

*Mother Goose looms behind the driver of the pony-drawn children's float bearing her name—one of seven children's floats built in the 1880s for the Barnum & London Circus.*

*The* Budweiser Beerwagon *is the only commercial vehicle in the Circus Parade. Pulled by the famous Budweiser Clydesdales, it is immensely popular. It was not unusual for local brewers and merchants to join in circus parades in the old days.*

*Left: The* France Bandwagon *was built in 1919 for the short-lived United States Motorized Circus. The sole survivor of a series of 16 tableau wagons, it is used in the Milwaukee parade as a bandwagon.*

*Manual street cleaners "clear the way" after the horses and before the oncoming marchers.*

The Circus World Museum's young giraffe is distracted by bottle feeding as it parades. *Ringling Bros. Giraffe Wagon is a replica of the original, built in 1893. The replica was completed in 1986 by a remarkable team of craftsmen at the museum.*

*Carin Cristiani parades her elephants in the 1988 circus celebration.*

Left: *The* Kangaroo Tableau Wagon *originated as a cage wagon on the Gollmar Bros. Circus sometime after 1910. (The Gollmar brothers, from Baraboo, Wisconsin, were first cousins to the Ringling brothers.) The Gollmar show was bought by James Patterson after the 1916 season and the wagon was used on his show through 1925— by which time it had been converted into a tableau wagon. Parade participants in Mexican costume are as novel as the painted kangaroos— and add to the lively mix of color and theme.*

*Built in 1903 for the Pawnee Bill Wild West Show, this bandwagon was one of the most popular ever used in circus parades. Note the unusually high "sky boards" above the wagon top. The vehicle weighs 5.5 tons.*

Built in Baraboo, Wisconsin, in 1892, the famous Ringling Bros. Circus' Bell Wagon *was originally publicized as displaying "The Bells of Moscow," although the bells were in fact cast in Milwaukee. It is said that John Ringling enjoyed hearing staid New England hymns played in a forthright manner by the bells on this striking vehicle. Here drawn by eight Clydesdales, the* Bell Wagon *still belongs to Ringling Bros. and Barnum & Bailey Circus and is on loan to the Circus World Museum.*

High wheels and light construction show that the Royal Italian Circus Bandwagon *was built for overland travel, probably in the 19th century. It was purchased by England's Fossett family after a small Italian touring circus failed during its tour of the British Isles.*

THE ROYAL ALIAN CIRCUS

Left: *The* Swan Bandwagon, *nicknamed the "Queen of Bandwagons," was built in 1907 by Henry Moeller, the famous wagon builder of Baraboo, Wisconsin. It was used by five different circuses and eventually at Disneyland before being acquired by the Circus World Museum.*

*Kay Rosaire's tiger poses atop a mirror ball during one of the circus performances during the Great Circus Parade weekend.*

*In the old days, elephants helped to erect the big top. Today, the tradition is still alive on the parade showgrounds.*

*Left: What is a circus parade without a circus? Different circuses are featured each year during the Great Circus Parade weekend. And part of the fun is watching the setting up of the big top.*

*This canine circus star is not actually "America's favorite dog catcher," but only one of his charges, shown here relaxing between performances in a patriotic environment.*

*For dromedaries, hot weather and a dusty lot are nothing to worry about. Chronic complainers, they give the impression of not liking anything in the first place.*

*Betsy Moore's exceptional trio of young Indian elephants are stars of the center ring under the parade ground's big top.*

*Kay Rosaire's Bengal tiger performs a classic leap through a fire hoop. To circus patrons in Milwaukee, the feat is impressive. For the tiger, it's just another exercise period.*

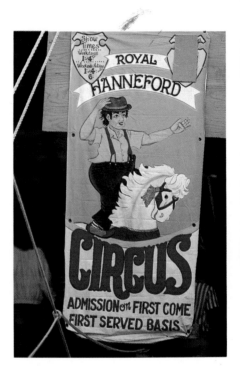

The Royal Hanneford Circus is one of many which have enlivened the festivities associated with the Great Circus Parade.

For children of any age, a visit to the circus lot is a highlight of the Great Circus Parade weekend, notwithstanding unexpected afternoon showers...

The king of beasts waits patiently in his historic den on wheels for the parade to begin.

A clown cop relaxes in his "safe" between circus performances.

*Detail of the Budweiser Beerwagon. Although this is a modern wagon, its craftsmanship is reminiscent of that seen on wagons built long ago.*

*This tiger attempts to live up to his billing as a dangerous wild animal in an old-time circus cage wagon. It is interesting to note that such cages are far more spacious than those generally in use today.*

*A canine performer proudly poses for a mug shot in the backstage area of the circus.*

*Just before parade time, a participant dressed in 18th-century garb minimizes the effects of sweltering heat with a cool, 20th-century drink...*

*...while a visitor does the same with the brew that made Milwaukee famous.*

Top: *A teamster poses with his horses—his pride and joy—beside Ringling Bros.'* Great Britain Bandwagon.

Left: *At the circus, old-timers are given special consideration on the parade weekend.*

Right: *A patched and tattered circus big top fails to dampen the holiday spirits of these elephant riders.*

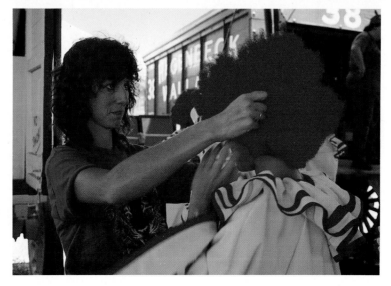

A teamster harnesses up for a trial run with his team.

It was with colorful posters such as these that the great circuses used to advertise their attractions.

Dressing for the parade. The virtually obligatory red fright wig is the crowning touch to the costume of this parade participant. The Circus World Museum's wardrobe department creates hundreds of circus costumes for each new edition of the Great Circus Parade.

Right: This is not what circus concessionaires refer to as a "pony sweep," at least not to the costumed rider. To her, it is the center ring beneath the big top—and she is the star!

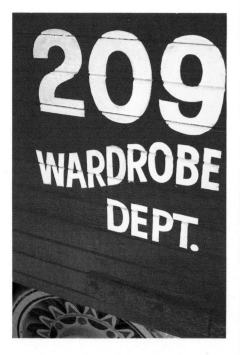

*Wardrobe Department Wagon No. 209 actually contains some of the innumerable costumes provided by the Circus World Museum. Many of them are created by Peggy Coburn, costume designer and wardrobe mistress of the museum.*

The success of the parade depends not only on the presence of circus wagons but also on the help of thousands of participants who contribute—in the parade itself, along its route, and behind the scenes—to make the great July weekend one of America's most popular and glorious events.

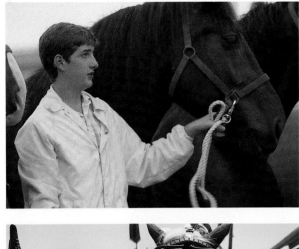

Coming with their handlers from many parts of the United States and Canada, 750 horses take part in the circus parade, either drawing the grand old circus wagons, or appearing in sections of the parade such as the "Mounted Ringling Equestriennes of 1908" and the "Madras Light Cavalry." But sometimes it takes a little urging to make equine stars get into the spirit of things . . .

*On the days before the parade, many attractions can occupy the attention of visitors, from a petting zoo to exercising horses, or watching seamstresses putting finishing touches on costumes and admiring the stables and immaculate harnesses, which are the pride of teamsters.*

*Details from* Asia, *one of four telescoping tableau wagons built by the Sebastian Wagon Works in New York City in 1902 for the Barnum & Bailey Circus. Unfortunately, the telescoping upper part of this wagon doesn't exist anymore; it was a large, gilded recumbent elephant surrounded by costumed figures. The series also included the* Africa Wagon, *which displayed a nearly life-size gilded camel and costumed attendants; the* Europe Wagon, *tipped by a large bull together with appropriately dressed human figures; and the* America Wagon, *which held an enormous bison and surrounding figures. Only* Asia *and* America—*the latter now a steam calliope—have survived.*

CHINA

PERSIA

AFGHAN

BORNEO

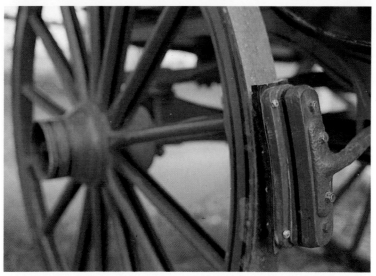

*Built in England in or before the 1860s, the handsome Bostock & Wombwell's Menagerie Bandwagon was restored in the Circus World Museum's shops for its first revival appearance at the 1988 Milwaukee Circus Parade, when it was drawn by eight Percherons in single file—a notably English style of hitch.*

Left: *Reflected memories. From left to right: Bostock & Wombwell's* Menagerie Bandwagon, Mother Goose *and* Cinderella *pony flots and the* Royal Italian Circus Bandwagon.

Several historic mechanical band-organs (such as Wurlitzer, Govioli and Limonaire) play continually amid the exotic circus wagons in the staging area for the parade.

This ORGAN
BUILT in 1909
at the WURLITZER factory
N.Tonawanda, N.Y.
Restored 1976
from the
Collection Cliff & Robbie Gray

*The* Old Woman in a Shoe *children's float, built in the 1880s for the* Barnum & London Circus *along with the* Mother Goose Float, *is reflected in a mirror that decorates* England's Twin Lions Telescoping Tableau Wagon.

*Detail from the elegant Sparks* Sea Serpent Tableau Wagon No. 33, *built for Sparks Circus around 1920.*

*Detail from the handsome woodcarving and painting which adorn the* Orchestmelochor, *a vehicle that paraded with the* Barnum & London Circus *in 1882.*

*The original of this* Elephant Tableau Bandwagon *appeared with the Sells-Floto Circus in 1915. The Circus World Museum applied the original side carvings to a brand-new reproduction of the original body.*

Originally built for the Sells & Downs Circus as a steam calliope in 1902 and later used by the Walter L. Main Circus, this wagon was changed to an air calliope between 1928 and 1930. It contains a band-organ that issues music through paper rolls.

The spectacular Golden Age of Chivalry Tableau Wagon *was built in New York City in 1902—3 by the Sebastian Wagon Company for the Barnum & Bailey Circus. When traveling on circus trains, the dragon's heads, wings and tail were removed and stored in the body of the wagon.*

Top right: *Although the great days of street parades were coming to a close in the 1920s, the Sells-Floto Cage Wagon No. 19 and some 25 others were built in the Peru, Indiana quarters of the American Circus Corporation. They were designed more for practicality than decorativeness. Multi-arch cages contained a chute along the inside rear for shifting animals in and out.*

The Star Tableau Wagon *usually carries an ornamented pedestal on its top level for circus beauties to pose on. Sometimes, as seen here, the pedestal is removed to facilitate presentation of large or more complex features. The telescoping tableau comes from Sir Robert Fossett's Circus in England, where it was built in the 19th century.*

*Voluptuous detail from the* Swan Bandwagon.

*Detail from England's* Gladiator Telescoping Tableau Wagon. *This magnificent wagon dates from the 1860s. It was donated to the Circus World Museum by Mary and Bailey Fossett, of the British circus family, but was originally used on "Lord" George Sanger's Circus. The* Asia Wagon *appears in the background.*

*One of the corner statues that gave the* Whiskers Cage Wagon *its name. Built in the early 1880s, it was with the Barnum & Bailey Circus on its European tour at the turn of the century.*

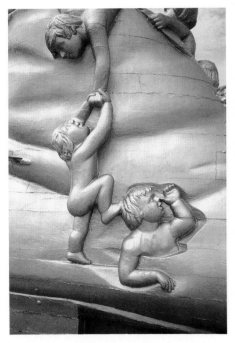

*Irreverent children adorn the* Old Woman in a Shoe *float, part of a series that also includes the* Mother Goose *and* Cinderella *floats.*

*Detail from the* Lion and Mirror Bandwagon.

*Cinderella and her Prince Charming traveled with the Barnum & London Circus in the mid-1880s as part of a children's section in the street parade. It was manufactured by the Sebastian Wagon Company. Also pictured: the* Sea Shell Tableau Wagon, *the* Ringling Bros. Circus Snake Den *and the* Cole Bros. Circus Air Calliope.

GREAT BRITAIN

Corner carving from the Barnum,
Bailey & Hutchinson Circus Cage
Wagon, *built by Fielding of New York
City in 1883.*

Left: *The Bode Wagon Works in
Cincinnati, Ohio, built the large* Great
Britain Bandwagon *for Ringling Bros.
Circus in 1902. The Ringlings were
attempting to outdo their competition,
the Barnum & Bailey Circus, which
had just returned from its triumphant
five-year tour of Europe. They actually
acquired the legendary circus in 1907.*

Portrait details of the
America Steam Calliope.

*This detail of the
flamboyant ornamentation
of the* Twin Lions
Telescoping Tableau
Wagon *denotes the
personal flamboyance of
its original owner, "Lord"
George Sanger.*

*Young visitors to the parade show-grounds enjoy a moment of rest in the shadow provided by the grand old circus wagons.* Top left: America Steam Calliope *and* Great Britain Bandwagon. Right: Star Tableau Wagon.

The venerable, old circus wagons offer inspiration to local artists visiting the parade's staging area. They sketch details of an Arthur Bros. Circus wagon originally built for the Hagenbeck-Wallace Circus (top left). The Great Britain Bandwagon No. 100 offers a seat from which to study the America Steam Calliope's carvings (center); and a superb wheel from the Columbia Bandwagon serves as back rest for another aspiring artist (right).

# The Great Circus Parade Order of March

(As given in *The Milwaukee Journal*, July 10, 1988)

The scope of the Great Circus Parade is difficult to imagine for those who have never witnessed it. Even photographs cannot give an accurate rendering of the gigantic procession, which lasts no less than two hours, from the Color Guard which opens the march, to the No. 200 *Signature Wagon* which closes it. This roster is given as an example, as the order and contents of the parade change each year. This is the official parade order of march for 1988.

| | |
|---|---|
| **Color Guard** | Milwaukee Metropolitan Noncommissioned Officers' Council. |
| The Old Guard Fife and Drum Corps | 3rd U.S. Army Infantry, Fort Myer, Virginia. |
| U.S. Navy Flag Unit | Recruit Training Command 50 State Flag Unit, Dept. of the Navy, Great Lakes Naval Training Center, Illinois. |
| U.S. Navy Band | Great Lakes Naval Training Center, Illinois. |
| U.S. Navy Marching Unit | Battleship USS *Wisconsin*, Pascagoula, Mississippi. |
| U.S. Coast Guard Precision & Marching Units | U.S. Coast Guard, Washington, D.C. |
| Cavalcade of Antique Automobiles | Organized by Walter Wilde and Bernie Peck, Milwaukee, Wisconsin. |
| Three Motorized Trolley Cars | Milwaukee County Transit System. |
| Police Patrol | Old-time police "paddy wagon" and policemen of the Milwaukee Police Post No. 415 of the American Legion. |
| 1927 Fire Engine | Milwaukee Fire Department and Milwaukee Fire Historical Society. |
| High-wheel Bikes of the 1890s | The **Wheelmen.** Leader: James Fienne, Racine, Wisconsin. |
| Six Men on a Bicycle | Jeff Rabas and "The Bachelors from Algoma," Algoma, Wisconsin. |
| Mounted Police Patrol | Twelve mounted police of the Wisconsin State Fair Park Mounted Police, West Allis, Wisconsin. |
| Fifth Wisconsin Volunteer Civil War Fife and Drums Corps | Milwaukee, Wisconsin. Leader: Ray Krawczyk. |
| Carriage | The Honorary Grand Marshal of the Great Circus Parade, Deloris Leuthold, Milwaukee, Wisconsin. Carriage and horses: John Fairclough, Sr., Paterson, New Jersey. |
| Carriage | Mayor John O. Norquist, City of Milwaukee, and his wife, Susan Mudd. Carriage and horses: Ann Leck, Wayzata, **Minnesota.** |
| Carriage | David F. Schulz, Milwaukee County Executive, and his wife, Joanne Schulz. Carriage and horses: Jay Hankee, Viroqua, Wisconsin. |
| Carriage | Senator Robert Kasten of Wisconsin, and his wife, Eva Kasten. Carriage and horses: Ned Hahn, Emerald, Wisconsin. |
| Milwaukee County Sheriff's Patrol | Six mounted sheriff's deputies and Milwaukee County Sheriff Richard E. Artison. |
| The Governor's Carriage | Carriage and horses: Ann Friend, Hartland, Wisconsin. |
| Introductory Wagon | Horses: Paul Stitt, Manitowoc, Wisconsin. |
| Lincoln-Way Community High School Marching Band | New Lenox, Illinois. Director: Randolph Kummer; Associate Director: Mark Joscher. |
| Carriage | Spuds MacKenzie and the "Spudettes," Anheuser-Busch Companies, Inc., St. Louis, Missouri. Carriage and horse: Art Pagel, Saukville, Wisconsin. |
| Mounted Flag Bearers | Nine riders and flag bearers from the Wisconsin Morgan Horse Club. |
| Ringling Bros. Circus Section Leaders | Two riders, Section Banner Carriers. |
| No. 87 Swan Bandwagon | Eight Belgian horses: William E. Hauser, Mindoro, Wisconsin. Many Happy Returns Circus Band. Director: Dick Strauss. |
| No. 20 Ringling Bros. Snake Den | Four Belgian horses: Sharon Riemer, Chilton, Wisconsin. The Humbert Family, Lombard, Wisconsin, and their giant boa constrictors. |
| The Field of the Cloth of Gold | Fifty horses and riders from the Wisconsin Morgan Horse Club, Wisconsin Horse Owners Alliance, and Kibler's Indian Summer Farm; dancers of the Milwaukee Ballet School. |
| Ringling Bros. Bell Wagon | Eight Clydesdale horses: Pat Morrison, Belle Plaine, Iowa. Carillonneur: Sara Roltgen, Baraboo, Wisconsin. |
| Ladies of the Ring Riding Side-Saddle | Three riders, the Hayes sisters, Baraboo, Wisconsin. One outrider horse and rider. |
| No. 84 Sea Shell Tableau Wagon | Six Belgian horses: Wayne Laursen, Rochester, Minnesota. Ladies of the Big Show. |
| No. 24 Terrell Jacobs Cage Wagon | Six ponies: Wayne Withers, Newark, Illinois. One lion cub, Clawdine. |
| Carriage | William Schuett, President and CEO of Security Savings & Loan Association, Milwaukee, Wisconsin. Carriage and horses: Art Pagel, Saukville, Wisconsin. |
| No. 1 Lion and Mirror Bandwagon | Eight Percheron horses: Harold Schumacher, Plainview, Minnesota. Old Mapleton Circus Band, Oconomowoc, Wisconsin. Leader: Gayle Pierce. |
| Mounted Ringling Equestriennes of 1908 | Sixteen horses and lady riders from the Wisconsin cities of Neenah, Menasha, Kewaskum, Eagle, Baraboo, Milwaukee, and the state of Iowa. |
| No. 73 Ringling Bros. Circus Hippopotamus Cage Wagon | Six horses. One hippopotamus furnished by Dave Hale, Cape Girardeau, Missouri. |

| | |
|---|---|
| No. 33 Sparks Circus Sea Serpent Tableau | Four Percheron horses: Ray Bast, Richfield, Wisconsin. |
| Grafton High School Marching Band | Grafton, Wisconsin. Director: Tom Christie. |
| Budweiser Beer Wagon and Famous Hitch | Eight Clydesdale horses. Anheuser-Busch Companies, Inc., St. Louis, Missouri. |
| Children's Section Introductory Banner | The Banner Carriers of the Baraboo High School Marching Band. |
| The Baraboo High School Marching Band | Baraboo, Wisconsin. Clown costumes by the Circus World Museum Wardrobe Department. Band directors: Rick Meiller and Greg Lang. |
| Mother Goose Float | Six ponies: Hartzell Bloomstrand, Dwight, Illinois. |
| The Old Woman Who Lives In A Shoe Float | Six ponies: Stanley Piper, Grant Park, Illinois. "Old Woman": Anna M. Allison, Wind Lake, Wisconsin. |
| Cinderella Float | Six ponies: Russell Runge, Menomonee Falls, Wisconsin. |
| No. 93 Giraffe Cage Wagon | Six Belgian horses: Lyle Getschman, Baraboo, Wisconsin. One giraffe: Circus World Museum. |
| Shades of Gentry Bros. Dog & Pony Shows of 1900 | Carriage and ponies: Donald Holthaus, Holmen, Wisconsin, Posing Dogs: Kenneth Krey, Loganville, Wisconsin. |
| St. George and the Dragon Wagon | Four lightweight horses: Harold Krueger, Sparta, Wisconsin. |
| No. 62 Columbia Bandwagon | Eight Clydesdale horses: DeVere Clay, Tomah, Wisconsin. Prof. Stich's Baraboo Circus Band, Baraboo, Wisconsin. Leader: Prof. Gerald Stich. |
| Clown Cart | Cart and pony: Happy the Clown (Jim Williams), from the Circus World Museum. |
| No. 19 Wolf Tableau Wagon | Miniature draft horses: Anthony Spruck, Milwaukee, Wisconsin. |
| No. 23 Terrell Jacobs Pony Cage Wagon | Six ponies: Harold Moritz, Minonk, Illinois. One leopard: Wille's Game Farm, Brandon, Wisconsin. |
| No. 14 Royal Italian Bandwagon | Eight ponies: Harold Moritz, Minonk, Illinois. Mel Hummitzsch Clown Band, Sheboygan, Wisconsin. |
| No. 44 Lion & Tiger Painted Tableau Wagon | Four Belgian horses: Elroy Brass, Elkhart Lake, Wisconsin. |
| Milwaukee's High Society | Clown on stilts: Walter Jankowski, Milwaukee, Wisconsin. |
| No. 85 Picture Frame Cage Wagon | Six Clydesdale horses: Robert Clay, Tomah, Wisconsin. Two lions: Jorge Barreda, animal trainer, Royal Hanneford Circus. |
| The Circus Mounted Band | Twenty musicians on horseback, Dr. Patricia Backhaus, Waukesha, Wisconsin. Horses: Al Gagliano, Eagle, Wisconsin. |
| Hagenbeck-Wallace Circus Cart | Harold Krueger, Sparta, Wisconsin. |
| No. 89 Beauty Tableau Wagon | Six Clydesdale horses: Dan Jones, Bangor, Wisconsin. |
| Clown and Mule | Brian Downes, Chicago, Illinois. |
| No. 82 Howe's Cage | Four Percheron horses: Lloyd Stoeklen, Menomonie, Wisconsin. One lion and trainers. |
| Carriage | Dr. H. Nicholas Muller III, Director of the State Historical Society of Wisconsin, and his wife, Carol Muller. Two Fjord horses and buggy: Paul Wasielewski, Eagle, Wisconsin. |
| No. 40 Schlitz Bandwagon | Eight Clydesdale horses: Merle Brooks, Westby, Wisconsin. Fifteen musicians, Dr. Spiro Mehail's Circus Band. |
| No. 26 Gollmar Bros. Mirror Bandwagon | Six Percheron horses: James Kruger, Aurora, Iowa. |
| South Milwaukee Senior High School Band | South Milwaukee, Wisconsin. Director: Sharon L. Awe. |
| No. 88 Whiskers Cage Wagon | Four Belgian horses: Earl Prochnow, Athens, Wisconsin. One lion and his trainer, Kay Rosaire, Sarasota, Florida. |
| Carriage | Passengers from Strong Funds of Milwaukee. Horses and carriage: Michael Crowley, Germantown, Wisconsin. |
| English Section Leaders | Two mounted riders. |
| Bostock & Wombwell's Menagerie Bandwagon | Eight Percheron horses in tandem: Merle Fischer, Jefferson, Wisconsin. Carl Ratzer's Brass Circus Band, Milwaukee, Wisconsin. |
| Lion & Gladiator Telescoping Tableau Wagon | Six Belgian horses: John Carlson, Henderson, Minnesota. |
| Twin Lions Telescoping Tableau Wagon | Six Belgian horses: Richard Savatski, Hartford, Wisconsin. |
| Star Tableau Wagon | Three Belgian horses (unicorn hitch): Dale Lockwood, Auburn, Indiana. |
| No. 100 Great Britain Bandwagon | Eight Percheron horses: Roy Fox, Lake Village, Indiana. Fifteen musicians, Lee Matthews' Great Circus Band, Milwaukee, Wisconsin. |
| Madras Light Cavalry | Ten riders and horses, Wasielewski Bar-W Stables, Eagle, Wisconsin. |
| No. 3 Royal Mail Coach | Four lightweight horses: Kenneth Koester, Scales Mounds, Illinois. |
| No. 12 Robbins Bros. Circus Cross Cage Wagon | Six ponies: Robert Michael and Fred Busse, Freeport and Esmond, Illinois. One cougar, Wille's Game Farm, Brandon, Wisconsin. |
| Carriage | Phillip Purpero, President of the Italian Community Center, Milwaukee, and his wife, Rose Mary Purpero. Carriage and horse: Michael Crowley, Germantown, Wisconsin. |
| No. 41 France Bandwagon | Six Belgian horses: Rolland Ruby, Brookfield, Wisconsin. Twelve musicians; Leader: Lee Peronto, Milwaukee, Wisconsin. |
| Joan of Arc | One mounted rider, Tracy Rafel, Union Grove, Wisconsin. |
| Mounted Knights in Shining Armor | Twelve horses and riders: Crystal Creek Riders, Beaver Dam, Wisconsin; Brill Riders, New Holstein, Wisconsin, and Juneau, Wisconsin. |

| | |
|---|---|
| The Golden Age of Chivalry Tableau | Six Percheron horses: Pete Lippitt, Woodstock, Georgia. |
| Waukesha North High School Marching Band | Waukesha, Wisconsin. Director: James Doepke. |
| Knights Templars of the Crusades | Horses and riders from the Menomonee Falls Saddle Club, Menomonee Falls, Wisconsin. |
| No. 22 Norris & Rowe Circus Tally Ho | Eight ponies: Otis Ruff, Streator, Illinois. |
| The Woodland String Band | Fifty musicians, Philadelphia, Pennsylvania. Transportation by Midwest Express Airlines. |
| Temple Tableau Wagon | Four Percheron horses: Robert Mischka, Whitewater, Wisconsin. (The wedding of Mary Jane Schmidt and Richard J. Percy, bandleader of the Circus World Museum, was actually performed on the wagon during the parade.) |
| Cart in Tandem | Cart and two horses in tandem hitch: Mary Ruth Marks, Verona, Wisconsin. |
| No. 19 Sells-Floto 3-Arch Cage Wagon | Six Percheron horses: Rich Lee, Hilbert, Wisconsin. Three tigers: Kay Rosaire, Sarasota, Florida. |
| No. 201 Adam Forepaugh Shows Stringer Stage Wagon | Six Percheron horses; Richard Koltz, Green Leaf, Wisconsin. Troupe of Clowns and Franz Jackson's Dixieland Band, Chicago, Illinois. |
| No. 31 Kangaroo Tableau Wagon | Four Clydesdale horses: Ralph Schwartz, Darlington, Wisconsin. |
| A High Class Clown | Clown Stilt Walker: Gary Soule, Sturgeon Bay, Wisconsin. |
| No. 25 Hagenbeck-Wallace 2-Arch Cage Wagon | Six Belgian horses: Keith Woodbury, Ridgeville, Indiana. Three lions: Jorge Barreda, Royal Hanneford Circus. |
| Wild West Section Leaders | Two mounted riders. |
| No. 80 Pawnee Bill Bandwagon and 20-Horse Hitch | Twenty Belgian horses: Paul Sparrow, Zearing, Iowa. Fifteen musicians, Art Zens Circus Band, Milwaukee, Wisconsin. |
| "Hon. William F. Cody" | Edwin Hill, LaCrosse, Wisconsin, portrays "Buffalo Bill." |
| Riders of the Old American West | |
| 101 Ranch Wild West Covered Wagon | Two oxen: Charles Robb, Arena, Wisconsin. |
| Lake Band of Milwaukee | Director: Mark Grauer. (A merger of several Milwaukee high school musicians into one summer marching band program.) |
| No. 98 Orchestmelochor Wagon | Six Clydesdale horses: Calvin Larson, Ripon, Wisconsin. American Indian riders: United Indians of Milwaukee. |
| A Band of Native American Indians | United Indians of Milwaukee. |
| No. 81 Howe's Cage Wagon | Four Belgian horses: Neil Kibler, Neenah, Wisconsin. One bear: Wille's Game Farm, Brandon, Wisconsin. |
| No. 116 Ken Maynard Air Calliope | Four Belgian horses: Lewis and Bud Schmidt, New Fane, Wisconsin. |
| Clown and Cart | Jolly the Clown (Art Petri), Milwaukee, Wisconsin. |
| No. 61 Barnum, Bailey & Hutchinson Tableau Cage Wagon | Three Belgian horses ("unicorn" hitch): Holden Hankee, Cashton, Wisconsin. |
| Korean Band | Myung Sook Chun Drum and Dance Ensemble, New York, New York. |
| No. 71 Asia Tableau Wagon | Eight Percheron horses: Art Eller, Pierz, Minnesota. Chinese costumed riders: Chinese-American Civic Club of Milwaukee, Wisconsin. |
| Chinese Ribbon Dancers | Twelve dancers. |
| Chinese Dragon | Twenty-six participants. |
| No. 23 Hagenbeck-Wallace 3-Arch Cage Wagon | Six Percheron horses: Ralph Coddington, Indianapolis, Indiana. Three lions: Kay Rosaire, Sarasota, Florida. |
| Continental Soldiers | Three mounted Continental Soldiers. |
| U.S. Marine Corps Band | Fourth Marine Aircraft Wing Band, U.S. Marine Corps, New Orleans, Louisiana. |
| Our Country Tableau Wagon | Four Belgian horses: Robert Ehnerd, Wrightstown, Wisconsin. Characters portrayed by look-alikes from Milwaukee and Baraboo, Wisconsin. |
| 132nd Army Band | Wisconsin Army National Guard, Madison, Wisconsin. |
| No. 206 Betsy Ross Tableau Wagon | Betsy Ross portrayed by Carol Skornicka, Madison, Wisconsin. |
| U.S. Air Force Band | Air Force Band of the Midwest, Chanute Air Force Base, Illinois. |
| No. 208 Statue of Liberty Tableau Wagon | Four Clydesdale horses: Gary Parrett, Stephenson, Minnesota. Miss Liberty: Colleen Burtts, Baraboo, Wisconsin; Honor Guard from the Milwaukee area. |
| No. 82 Cole Bros. Circus Unafon Wagon | Six ponies: Dean Baldwin, Alma, Wisconsin. Instrumentalist: Rich Crabtree, Milwaukee, Wisconsin. |
| Camels | Dave Hale, Cape Girardeau, Missouri. |
| No. 181 Al G. Barnes Elephant Tableau Wagon | Six Percheron horses: Soder Farms, Three Lakes, Wisconsin. |
| Mounted Elephant Crier | Harry Vosekuil, Beaver Dam, Wisconsin. |
| Three Herds of Circus Elephants | Elephants provided by: George Carden, Springfield, Missouri; Bucky Steel, Seagoville, Texas; Carin Cristiani, Sarasota, Florida. |
| No. 72 America Steam Calliope | Eight Percheron horses: William Farmer, Eaton, Ohio. Instrumentalist: Herbert Head, Detroit, Michigan. |
| No. 200 Signature Wagon | Two Belgian horses; Muriel Finch, Tomah, Wisconsin. |

# Circus World Museum Proudly Presents the Great Circus Parade

Sunday, July 16, 1989

As this book goes to press, preparations are well under way for the 1989 Great Circus Parade. Here is the tentative parade order at the time of printing. This list is subject to change at any time right up to and during parade day, July 16, 1989.

Introductory Wagon
Marching Band
Mounted Flag Bearers

## Ringling Bros. Section

Ringling Bros. Circus Section Leaders
No. 87 Swan Bandwagon
Carriage
No. 20 Ringling Bros. Snake Den
Marching Band
Rainbow Equestriennes
Ringling Bros. Bell Wagon
No. 73 Ringling Bros. Circus Hippopotamus Cage Wagon
Mounted Ringling Equestriennes of 1908
No. 93 Giraffe Cage Wagon
No. 84 Sea Shell Tableau Wagon
No. 1 Lion and Mirror Bandwagon

Carriage
Budweiser Beer Wagon and Famous Clydesdale Hitch

## Children's Section

Children's Section Introductory Banner
Baraboo High School Marching Band
Mother Goose Float
Gentry Bros. Dog & Pony Shows (Posing Dogs)
Old Woman Who Lives In A Shoe Float
No. 82 Cole Bros. Circus Unafon Wagon
Red Clown Cart — Art Pagel
No. 82 Howe's Cage (yellow)
Hagenbeck-Wallace Circus Cart
No. 26 Gollmar Bros. Mirror Bandwagon
No. 33 Sparks Circus Sea Serpent Tableau
Milwaukee's High Society (clown on stilts)

No. 23 Terrell Jacobs Pony Cage Wagon (blue)
Clown and Mule
No. 83 Barnum & Bailey Tableau Cage Wagon
Marching Band
Carriage
No. 88 Whiskers Cage Wagon

Cleopatra in Sedan Chair, two Camels
Temple Tableau with Handmaidens to the Queen
   (Twelve- to eighteen-camel hitch, six camel outriders)
Marching Band

## English Section

English Section Banner Carriers and Leaders
Bostock & Wombwell's Menagerie Bandwagon
Lion & Gladiator Telescoping Tableau Wagon
No. 3 Royal Mail Coach
Star Tableau Wagon
Twin Lions Telescoping Tableau Wagon
No. 22 Norris & Rowe Circus Tally Ho
Mounted Band

## Wild West Section

Wild West Section Leaders
Hon. William F. Cody — "Buffalo Bill"
Riders of the Old American West
No. 80 Pawnee Bill Bandwagon
101 Ranch Wild West Covered Wagon
No. 24 Terrell Jacobs Cage Wagon (yellow)
   (Ten-miniature donkey hitch)
No. 116 Ken Maynard Air Calliope
No. 98 Orchestmelochor Wagon
A Band of Native American Indians
Cossack Marching Band
Carriage
No. 29 Sells-Floto Leopard Cage
No. 44 Lion & Tiger Painted Tableau Wagon
No. 40 Schlitz Bandwagon
No. 81 Howe's Cage Wagon (orange)
No. 11 Charging Tiger Tableau

Waukesha North High School Marching Band
No. 31 Kangaroo Tableau Wagon
High Class Clown (clown on stilts)
No. 12 Robbins Bros. Circus Cross Cage Wagon

## Congress of Nations Section

Marching Band
Two Hemispheres Bandwagon (Forty-horse hitch)
Carriage
No. 71 Asia Tableau Wagon
Carriage
Royal Italian Bandwagon
Joan of Arc
Mounted Knights in Shining Armor
No. 41 France Bandwagon
The Field of the Cloth of Gold
No. 62 Columbia Bandwagon
St. George and the Dragon Wagon
Ladies of the Ring Riding Side-Saddle
No. 100 Great Britain Bandwagon
No. 61 Barnum, Bailey & Hutchinson Tableau Cage Wagon

## Patriotic Section

Patriotic Section Leaders — Continental Soldiers
U.S. Marine Corps Band
No. 206 Betsy Ross Tableau Wagon
No. 89 Beauty Tableau Wagon
Fourth Army U.S. Army Band
Our Country Tableau Wagon
U.S. Air Force Band of the Midwest
No. 201 Adam Forepaugh Shows Stringer Stage Wagon
   (Lou Ann Jacob and her baby African elephants)
Elephant & Howdah: Herd of Circus Elephants (Bobby Moore)
No. 181 Al G. Barnes Elephant Tableau Wagon
   (Four-elephant hitch — Bobby Moore)
No. 72 America Steam Calliope

No. 200 Signature Wagon

# Index